RESILIENCE BEYOND ADVERSITY

Harnessing Motivation For Personal Growth

RESILIENCE BEYOND ADVERSITY

Copyright © 2024

All rights reserved.

Table Of Contents

Chapter 1: Fueling the Fire Within..1

    Recognizing Your Passions and Dreams..1

    Overcoming Self-Doubt and Fear 4

    Finding Inspiration in Everyday Life 7

    Setting Compelling Goals: The Blueprint for Success 10

    Creating a Vision Board for Motivation 13

Chapter 2: The Mindset Advantage 20

    Understanding the Power of Mindset..20

    Identifying and Challenging Limiting Beliefs..................................23

    Practicing Positive Self-Talk and Affirmations 25

    Cultivating Resilience in the Face of Setbacks 29

    Adopting a Growth Mindset for Continuous Improvement 31

    Visualizing Success and Manifesting Your Goals 33

Chapter 3: Cultivate Positivity 36

    Gratitude Practices for Daily Life 36

    Keeping a Gratitude Journal...38

    Surrounding Yourself with Positive Influences 40

    Letting Go of Negativity and Resentment..41

    Finding Silver Linings in Challenges 43

Spreading Kindness and Compassion to Others 45

Chapter 4: Journey of Reflection 48

Reflecting on Past Achievements and Failures 48

Clarifying Your Values and Priorities 50

Identifying What Truly Matters to You 52

Exploring Your Passions and Interests 54

Reconnecting with Your Inner Child and Authentic Self 56

Setting Intentions for Future Growth and Development 58

Chapter 5: The Rhythm of Routine 62

Incorporating Exercise and Movement into Your Daily Life 65

Creating a Healthy Work-Life Balance 68

Setting Boundaries to Protect Your Energy 70

Developing a Nighttime Routine for Restful Sleep 72

Chapter 6: Triumph in Every Step 75

Celebrating Small Wins and Milestones 75

Acknowledging Your Progress and Growth 77

Rewarding Yourself for Achievements 78

Sharing Your Successes with Others 80

Learning from Setbacks and Challenges 82

Cultivating Resilience and Perseverance in the Face of Adversity
.... 84

Chapter 7: Faith in Action 87

Finding Strength and Comfort in Prayer and Meditation 89

Trusting in Divine Timing and Universal Guidance 91

Letting Go of Control and Surrendering to the Flow of Life 92

Finding Meaning and Purpose in Life's Challenges........................94

Connecting with a Community of Like-Minded Individuals for Support and Encouragement 96

CONCLUSION **98**

Author Biography..**99**

Chapter 1:
Fueling the Fire Within

Recognizing Your Passions and Dreams

Passions and dreams are the fuel that propels us forward in life, driving us towards fulfillment and success. However, recognizing these passions and dreams is not always a straightforward process. It requires introspection, exploration, and a willingness to listen to the whispers of our hearts. This first section of chapter 1 will talk on the importance of recognizing your passions and dreams and explore practical strategies for uncovering them.

Understanding the Significance

Your passions and dreams are the essence of who you are. They represent your deepest desires—the things that ignite a fire within you and fill you with purpose and excitement. When you align your life with your passions and dreams, you experience a sense of alignment and fulfillment that transcends material success.

Reflecting on Your Interests and Activities

One of the first steps in recognizing your passions and dreams is to reflect on your interests and activities. What activities do you find yourself drawn to? What subjects or topics captivate your attention? Take some time to make a list of the things that bring you joy and fulfillment, no matter how big or small.

Paying attention to your emotions

Your emotions can provide valuable clues about your passions and dreams. Pay attention to how you feel when you're engaged in different activities or pursuits. Do you feel energized and enthusiastic, or do you feel drained and uninspired? Your emotional responses can help guide you towards activities that align with your true passions.

Exploring new opportunities

Don't be afraid to step outside of your comfort zone and explore new opportunities. Trying new things allows you to discover hidden passions and talents that you may not have been aware of.

Whether it's taking up a new hobby, volunteering for a cause you're passionate about, or traveling to new places, embrace opportunities for growth and exploration.

Asking Yourself Thought-Provoking Questions

Asking yourself thought-provoking questions can help stimulate introspection and uncover deeper layers of your passions and dreams.

Consider questions such as:

- What would I do if money were no object?
- What activities make me lose track of time?
- What legacy do I want to leave behind?

- What am I truly passionate about?

Seeking Inspiration from Others

Inspiration can often be found in the stories and experiences of others. Seek out mentors, role models, and individuals who are living their passions and dreams. Learn from their journeys, glean insights from their successes and failures, and allow their stories to ignite your own sense of purpose and possibility.

Embracing Your Unique Journey

Remember that your journey towards recognizing your passions and dreams is unique to you. Embrace the twists and turns, the highs and lows, and trust that each experience is guiding you towards greater clarity and alignment. Be patient with yourself and trust in the process of self-discovery.

Taking Action

Ultimately, recognizing your passions and dreams is only the first step. It's important to take action and pursue them wholeheartedly. Set goals, make plans, and take concrete steps towards turning your dreams into reality. Remember that the journey may be challenging at times, but the rewards of living a life aligned with your passions are immeasurable.

Recognizing your passions and dreams is a deeply personal and empowering process. By reflecting on your interests, listening to your emotions, exploring new opportunities, asking thought-provoking questions, seeking inspiration from others, and embracing your unique journey, you can unlock the full potential of your life and create a future filled with meaning, purpose, and fulfillment.

Overcoming Self-Doubt and Fear

Self-doubt and fear are two of the most common barriers standing between individuals and their dreams. They can paralyze us, keeping us stuck in a cycle of hesitation and insecurity. However, by understanding the roots of these emotions and implementing strategies to overcome them, we can unlock our full potential and pursue our goals with confidence and conviction.

Understanding Self-Doubt and Fear

Self-doubt is the voice of uncertainty that whispers in our minds, questioning our abilities and worthiness. It often stems from past experiences, negative self-talk, and comparison to others. Fear, on the other hand, is the primal instinct that arises in the face of perceived danger or risk. While self-doubt focuses on our internal doubts and insecurities, fear is often triggered by external threats or challenges.

The Impact of Self-Doubt and Fear

Self-doubt and fear can have profound effects on every aspect of our lives. They can hold us back from pursuing our dreams, taking risks, and seizing opportunities. They can erode our self-confidence, leading to feelings of inadequacy and unworthiness. Left unchecked, self-doubt and fear can limit our potential and prevent us from living fulfilling and meaningful lives.

Challenging Limiting Beliefs

The first step in overcoming self-doubt and fear is to challenge the limiting beliefs that fuel them. Take a closer look at the thoughts and beliefs that contribute to your feelings of doubt and fear. Are they based on facts, or are they distorted perceptions? Question the validity of these beliefs and replace them with more empowering and supportive thoughts.

Cultivating Self-Compassion

Self-compassion is the antidote to self-doubt and fear. Treat yourself with the same kindness and understanding that you would offer to a friend facing similar challenges. Acknowledge your humanity and imperfections, and remind yourself that it's okay to make mistakes and experience setbacks. By practicing self-compassion, you can quiet the voice of self-doubt and foster a greater sense of confidence and resilience.

Stepping outside your comfort zone

Courage is not the absence of fear but the willingness to act in spite of it. Challenge yourself to step outside your comfort zone and confront your fears head-on. Start with small, manageable tasks and gradually work your way up to bigger challenges. Each time you push past your comfort zone, you'll expand your confidence and prove to yourself that you're capable of more than you ever imagined.

Visualizing Success

Visualization is a powerful tool for overcoming self-doubt and fear. Take some time each day to visualize yourself succeeding in your goals and overcoming obstacles. Imagine yourself feeling confident, capable, and empowered as you navigate challenges and achieve success. By repeatedly visualizing positive outcomes, you'll reprogram your subconscious mind and build a strong belief in your abilities.

Seeking Support

Don't be afraid to reach out for support when you're struggling with self-doubt and fear. Surround yourself with positive, encouraging people who believe in you and your abilities. Lean on friends, family members, mentors, and coaches who can offer guidance, perspective, and encouragement. Remember that you don't have to face your challenges alone.

Taking Action Despite Fear

The most effective way to overcome self-doubt and fear is to take action despite them. Instead of waiting for your fears to dissipate before taking action, choose to act courageously in spite of them. Break your goals down into smaller, manageable steps and focus on taking consistent action towards them. As you take action, you'll build momentum and confidence, making it easier to push through your fears.

Celebrating Your Progress

Finally, don't forget to celebrate your progress along the way. Acknowledge and celebrate each step forward, no matter how small. Celebrating your progress reinforces your belief in yourself and your ability to overcome challenges. It also provides motivation and momentum to continue moving forward on your journey.

Self-doubt and fear are natural aspects of the human experience, but they don't have to hold you back from living a fulfilling and meaningful life. By understanding the roots of these emotions, challenging limiting beliefs, cultivating self-compassion, stepping outside your comfort zone, visualizing success, seeking support, taking action despite fear, and celebrating your progress, you can overcome self-doubt and fear and unlock your full potential. Remember, courage is not the absence of fear but the willingness to act in spite of it. Embrace your courage, believe in yourself, and pursue your dreams with confidence and conviction.

Finding Inspiration in Everyday Life

Inspiration is all around us, waiting to be discovered in the ordinary moments of our daily lives. Whether it's the beauty of nature, the kindness of a stranger, or the wisdom of a friend, there are endless sources of inspiration just waiting to be tapped into.

Cultivating Awareness

The first step in finding inspiration in everyday life is to cultivate awareness. Slow down and take notice of the world around you. Pay attention to the sights, sounds, smells, and sensations that surround you. By becoming more present and mindful, you'll open yourself up to the beauty and wonder that exist in even the most mundane moments.

Connecting with Nature

Nature is a powerful source of inspiration, offering endless opportunities for reflection, awe, and wonder. Take time to immerse yourself in the natural world, whether it's going for a walk in the woods, watching the sunrise, or simply sitting outside and feeling the sun on your face. Allow yourself to be captivated by the beauty and tranquility of nature, and let it inspire you to create and explore.

Seeking novel experiences

Routine can be comforting, but it can also be stifling to creativity and inspiration. Shake things up by seeking out new experiences and adventures. Visit a museum or art gallery, try a new hobby or activity, or explore a different neighborhood or city. Stepping outside of your comfort zone and exposing yourself to new ideas and perspectives can spark fresh inspiration and ignite your passion for life.

Embracing Curiosity

Curiosity is the fuel that drives inspiration. Cultivate a curious mindset by asking questions, seeking answers, and exploring the unknown. Be open to new ideas, perspectives, and possibilities, and allow yourself to follow your curiosity wherever it may lead. Remember that inspiration often comes from unexpected places, so stay curious and keep an open mind.

Finding beauty in the ordinary

Inspiration doesn't always have to come from grand gestures or extraordinary events. Sometimes, the most profound inspiration can be found in the simple moments of everyday life. Take time to appreciate the small pleasures and beauties that surround you, whether it's the laughter of children, the warmth of a cup of tea, or the colors of a sunset. By finding beauty in the ordinary, you'll cultivate a deeper sense of gratitude and inspiration.

Connecting with others

Humans are social beings, and our connections with others can be a rich source of inspiration. Surround yourself with people who uplift and inspire you, whether it's friends, family members, or mentors. Engage in meaningful conversations, share ideas and experiences, and draw inspiration from the unique perspectives and insights of those around you. Remember that we are all connected and that by building strong relationships with others, we can inspire and be inspired in return.

Practicing Gratitude

Gratitude is a powerful practice that can cultivate a sense of wonder and appreciation for life. Take time each day to reflect on the things you're grateful for, whether it's the love of family and friends, the beauty of nature, or the opportunities that life has afforded you. By focusing on the positive aspects of your life, you'll cultivate a mindset of abundance and inspiration that will fuel your creative endeavors.

Finding meaning and purpose

Ultimately, inspiration is deeply connected to our sense of meaning and purpose in life. Take time to reflect on what truly matters to you and what gives your life meaning and fulfillment. Whether it's pursuing your passions, making a difference in the lives of others, or living in alignment with your values, finding meaning and purpose can provide a powerful source of inspiration that fuels your creativity and drives you forward.

Inspiration is not a rare commodity reserved for artists, poets, and visionaries. It's a natural and abundant resource that exists within each of us, waiting to be discovered and unleashed. By cultivating awareness, connecting with nature, seeking novel experiences, embracing curiosity, finding beauty in the ordinary, connecting with others, practicing gratitude, and finding meaning and purpose, you can tap into the endless wellspring of inspiration that exists within you and in the world around you. So go ahead, open your eyes, open your heart, and let inspiration guide you on your journey of creativity, passion, and purpose.

Setting Compelling Goals: The Blueprint for Success

Setting goals is the cornerstone of success. Whether you're striving for personal growth, professional advancement, or simply looking to improve your quality of life, having clear and compelling goals gives you direction, purpose, and motivation.

Understanding the Power of Goals

Goals serve as a roadmap for your journey through life. They provide clarity about what you want to achieve and create a framework for taking purposeful action. Without goals, you may find yourself drifting aimlessly, lacking direction and focus. Setting compelling goals gives you something to strive for, igniting your passion and propelling you forward even in the face of challenges.

The Characteristics of Compelling Goals

Compelling goals possess several key characteristics that set them apart from ordinary objectives. Firstly, they are specific and measurable, clearly defining what you want to accomplish and how you'll know when you've achieved it. Secondly, compelling goals are challenging yet achievable, stretching your abilities and pushing you outside your comfort zone. Thirdly, they are relevant to your values, passions, and long-term aspirations, aligning with your vision for the future. Lastly, compelling goals are time-bound, setting deadlines and milestones to keep you accountable and focused.

The Importance of Clarity and Specificity

Clarity is essential when setting goals. Vague, ambiguous goals are difficult to pursue and easy to abandon. Instead, aim for clarity and specificity in defining your objectives. Break down your goals into smaller, actionable steps, and be precise about what you want to accomplish and why it matters to you. The clearer your vision, the easier it will be to create a plan and stay motivated.

The Power of Visualization

Visualization is a powerful tool for goal setting. Take time to visualize yourself achieving your goals in vivid detail. Imagine what it will look, feel, and sound like when you reach your objectives. Visualizing success activates your subconscious mind, aligning your thoughts and actions with your desired outcomes. By regularly visualizing your goals, you'll reinforce your commitment and increase your chances of success.

Creating SMART Goals

SMART is an acronym that stands for Specific, Measurable, Achievable, Relevant, and Time-bound. When setting goals, strive to make them SMART. Specific goals are clear and well-defined, measurable goals are quantifiable and trackable, achievable goals are realistic and within reach; relevant goals align with your values and priorities; and time-bound goals have deadlines and milestones to keep you on track. By applying the SMART criteria to your goal-setting process, you'll increase your likelihood of success and ensure that your goals are both compelling and attainable.

Setting Goals in Different Areas of Your Life

Goals are not limited to one area of your life; they can encompass various aspects, including career, finances, health, relationships, personal development, and leisure. Take time to assess each area of your life and identify areas where you'd like to see improvement or growth. Set goals that reflect your priorities and aspirations in each domain, creating a balanced and holistic approach to goal-setting.

The Importance of Accountability and Tracking Progress

Accountability is crucial when it comes to goal achievement. Share your goals with trusted friends, family members, or mentors who can support and encourage you on your journey. Additionally, track your progress regularly, celebrating your successes and adjusting your approach as needed. Accountability and progress tracking help keep you motivated and focused, ensuring that you stay committed to your goals even when faced with obstacles or setbacks.

Overcoming Obstacles and Staying Motivated

Achieving your goals is rarely a linear path. Along the way, you may encounter obstacles, setbacks, and challenges that test your resolve. During these times, it's essential to stay resilient and keep your eye on the prize. Cultivate a growth mindset, view setbacks as learning opportunities, and remain flexible in your approach. Additionally, stay connected to your "why"—the deeper purpose behind your goals—and draw inspiration from your vision for the future. By staying resilient, adaptable, and focused on your goals, you'll overcome obstacles and ultimately achieve success.

Setting compelling goals is the blueprint for success in any area of life. By defining clear, specific, and meaningful objectives, creating a plan of action, and staying committed and focused, you can turn your dreams into reality. Remember to make your goals SMART, set them in various areas of your life, hold yourself accountable, and stay resilient in the face of challenges. With determination, perseverance, and a clear vision, you can achieve anything you set your mind to.

Creating a Vision Board for Motivation

A vision board is a powerful tool for manifesting your dreams and goals. It's a visual representation of your aspirations, desires, and intentions, designed to inspire and motivate you towards their achievement. By bringing your dreams to life through images, words, and symbols, you activate the law of attraction and align your thoughts and actions with your desired outcomes.

Understanding the Purpose of a Vision Board

A vision board serves as a tangible reminder of your goals and dreams. It provides a visual anchor that keeps you focused and motivated, even when faced with challenges or setbacks. By regularly viewing your vision board, you reinforce your commitment to your goals and cultivate a positive mindset that attracts opportunities and resources to support your journey.

Gathering Inspiration and Materials

Before you begin creating your vision board, take some time to gather inspiration and materials. Browse magazines, websites, and social media platforms for images and quotes that resonate with your goals and aspirations. Consider including photographs, drawings, affirmations, and symbols that evoke positive emotions and reflect your vision for the future. Additionally, gather materials such as a poster board, glue, scissors, markers, and any other supplies you'll need to bring your vision board to life.

Clarifying Your Goals and Intentions

Before you start arranging your vision board, take some time to clarify your goals and intentions. What do you want to achieve? What areas of your life do you want to focus on? Be specific and intentional about what you include on your vision board, choosing images and words that align with your deepest desires and aspirations. Whether it's career success, financial abundance, vibrant health, loving relationships, or personal growth, ensure that your vision board reflects your most important goals and intentions.

Creating Your Vision Board

Once you have your materials and goals clarified, it's time to start creating your vision board. Begin by laying out your images, quotes, and symbols on the poster board, arranging them in a way that feels visually pleasing and meaningful to you. Get creative and experiment with different layouts and compositions until you find one that resonates with your vision. As you work, stay connected to the emotions and feelings associated with your goals, allowing them to guide your choices and decisions.

Visualizing Success and Manifesting Your Goals

As you create your vision board, take time to visualize yourself achieving your goals and manifesting your dreams. Close your eyes and imagine what it will look, feel, and sound like when you reach your desired outcomes. Visualize yourself living the life you've always dreamed of, experiencing joy, fulfillment, and abundance in every area of your life. By consistently visualizing success, you activate the law of attraction and align your subconscious mind with your desired outcomes, making them more likely to manifest in your reality.

Displaying and Using Your Vision Board

Once your vision board is complete, find a prominent place to display it where you'll see it every day. This could be in your bedroom, office, or any other space where you spend a lot of time.

Make it a habit to spend a few minutes each day reviewing your vision board, focusing on the images and words that inspire you and remind you of your goals. You can also use your vision board as a visualization tool during meditation or visualization exercises, allowing yourself to fully immerse yourself in the feelings and emotions associated with your desired outcomes.

Updating and Revising Your Vision Board

Your goals and aspirations may evolve over time, so it's important to regularly update and revise your vision board to reflect these changes. As you achieve goals or set new ones, replace old images and quotes with new ones that align with your current desires and intentions. Keep your vision board fresh and relevant, ensuring that it continues to inspire and motivate you towards your ever-expanding vision for the future.

Creating a vision board is a powerful tool for motivation and manifestation. By visually representing your goals and desires, you activate the law of attraction and align your thoughts and actions with your desired outcomes. Whether you're striving for career success, financial abundance, vibrant health, loving relationships, or personal growth, a vision board can help you stay focused, inspired, and motivated on your journey towards success. So gather your materials, clarify your goals, and start creating your vision board today. Your dreams are waiting to be brought to life.

Seeking Guidance from Mentors and Role Models

One of the most effective ways to navigate life's challenges and achieve success is by seeking guidance from mentors and role models. These individuals have walked the path before us, gained valuable experience, and can offer insights, advice, and support to help us on our journey. Whether you're pursuing personal growth, professional development, or simply looking for inspiration, connecting with mentors and role models can be a game-changer in achieving your goals.

The Importance of Mentorship

Mentorship is a relationship in which a more experienced or knowledgeable individual provides guidance, support, and advice to a less experienced person. Mentors offer valuable insights, share their wisdom and expertise, and help mentees navigate challenges and overcome obstacles. By learning from the experiences of others, mentees can accelerate their growth, expand their perspectives, and avoid common pitfalls on their path to success.

Finding the right mentor

Finding the right mentor is a crucial step in the mentorship process. Look for individuals who have achieved success in your desired field or area of interest and who possess qualities and values that resonate with you. Consider reaching out to professionals in your network, attending networking events, or joining mentorship programs or organizations to connect with potential mentors. When approaching potential mentors, be respectful of their time and expertise, and clearly articulate what you hope to gain from the mentorship relationship.

Building a Relationship with Your Mentor

Once you've found a mentor, focus on building a strong and meaningful relationship. Take the initiative to schedule regular meetings or check-ins and come prepared with specific questions or topics for discussion. Be open and receptive to feedback, and demonstrate a willingness to learn and grow. Show appreciation for your mentor's guidance and support, and look for ways to add value to the relationship. Remember that mentorship is a two-way street, and both parties should benefit from the exchange of knowledge and experience.

Learning from role models

In addition to seeking guidance from mentors, it's also valuable to learn from role models—individuals who inspire and embody the qualities and characteristics you aspire to emulate. Role models can be public figures, historical figures, or individuals in your personal or professional network who have achieved success in areas you admire. Study their lives, actions, and achievements, and identify the traits and behaviors that contribute to their success. By modeling your behavior after your role models, you can cultivate similar qualities and accelerate your own growth and development.

Seeking inspiration and motivation

Mentors and role models not only offer practical guidance and advice but also serve as a source of inspiration and motivation. Their stories of overcoming obstacles, achieving success, and making a difference in the world can ignite your passion and fuel your drive to pursue your goals. Surround yourself with positive influences and seek out opportunities to learn from those who have achieved what you aspire to accomplish. By immersing yourself in the wisdom and inspiration of mentors and role models, you'll stay motivated and focused on your path to success.

Giving Back and Paying It Forward

As you benefit from the guidance and support of mentors and role models, don't forget to pay it forward and give back to others. Share your knowledge, experiences, and insights with those who are earlier in their journey, and offer guidance and support to help them succeed. By serving as a mentor or role model to others, you'll not only make a positive impact on their lives but also reinforce your own learning and growth. Remember that mentorship is a reciprocal relationship, and both mentors and mentees can benefit from the exchange of knowledge and support.

Seeking guidance from mentors and role models is a powerful strategy for achieving success and personal growth. Mentors offer valuable insights, support, and advice to help navigate challenges and overcome obstacles, while role models inspire and motivate us to reach our full potential. By building meaningful relationships with mentors, learning from role models, and giving back to others, we can accelerate our growth, expand our perspectives, and achieve our goals with confidence and clarity. So don't hesitate to reach out to mentors and role models who can help you on your journey; the guidance and support you receive can make all the difference in your success.

Chapter 2:
The Mindset Advantage

Understanding the Power of Mindset

The power of mindset cannot be overstated. Your mindset, or your attitude and beliefs about yourself and the world, shapes every aspect of your life, from your relationships and career to your health and happiness. By cultivating a positive and growth-oriented mindset, you can unlock your full potential, overcome challenges, and create the life you desire.

Fixed vs. growth mindset

There are two primary types of mindsets: fixed and growth. Individuals with a fixed mindset believe that their abilities, talents, and intelligence are fixed traits that cannot be changed. They may avoid challenges, give up easily, and see failure as a reflection of their inherent abilities. In contrast, those with a growth mindset believe that their abilities can be developed through dedication, effort, and learning. They embrace challenges, persist in the face of obstacles, and see failure as an opportunity for growth and learning.

The Impact of Mindset on Success

Your mindset plays a significant role in determining your success and fulfillment in life. Research has shown that individuals with a growth mindset are more likely to achieve their goals, perform better in school and work, and experience greater levels of happiness and well-being. This is because a growth mindset fosters resilience, perseverance, and a willingness to learn and adapt in the face of adversity. By cultivating a growth mindset, you can overcome setbacks, bounce back from failure, and ultimately achieve your full potential.

Shifting your mindset

If you find yourself stuck in a fixed mindset, it's never too late to make a change. Shifting your mindset is a process that requires self-awareness, intention, and practice. Start by paying attention to your thoughts and beliefs, particularly when faced with challenges or setbacks. Notice any negative or limiting beliefs that arise, and challenge them with more empowering and growth-oriented thoughts. Remind yourself that failure is not a reflection of your abilities but an opportunity for growth and learning. Surround yourself with people who embody a growth mindset and who inspire and support you on your journey.

Cultivating a growth mindset

There are several strategies you can use to cultivate a growth mindset and harness the power of your mind to achieve your goals. One strategy is to embrace challenges and see them as opportunities for growth and learning. Instead of avoiding difficult tasks, lean into them and approach them with curiosity and enthusiasm. Another strategy is to persist in the face of obstacles and setbacks. Instead of giving up at the first sign of failure, use setbacks as a springboard for growth and keep moving forward. Additionally, seek out opportunities for learning and development, whether through formal education, self-study, or mentorship. By continuously expanding your knowledge and skills, you'll strengthen your belief in your ability to grow and succeed.

The Role of Positive Thinking

Positive thinking is another powerful tool for cultivating a growth mindset. By focusing on the positive aspects of a situation and maintaining an optimistic outlook, you can increase your resilience, motivation, and overall well-being. Practice gratitude daily by reflecting on the things you're thankful for and appreciating the blessings in your life. Surround yourself with positive influences, whether it's uplifting books, inspiring music, or supportive friends and family members. By cultivating a positive mindset, you'll create a fertile environment for growth and success in all areas of your life.

The power of mindset is undeniable. By cultivating a growth mindset and harnessing the power of positive thinking, you can overcome challenges, achieve your goals, and create a life of fulfillment and purpose. Remember that your mindset is not fixed; it's a choice you make every day. Choose to embrace challenges, persist in the face of obstacles, and maintain an optimistic outlook, and you'll unleash the full potential of your mind to create the life you desire.

Identifying and Challenging Limiting Beliefs

Limiting beliefs are deeply ingrained thoughts and beliefs that hold us back from reaching our full potential. They are often rooted in fear, self-doubt, or past experiences and can manifest as negative self-talk, self-sabotaging behaviors, and a lack of confidence. By identifying and challenging these limiting beliefs, we can break free from their grip and create a life of abundance, success, and fulfillment.

Recognizing Limiting Beliefs

The first step in overcoming limiting beliefs is to recognize them for what they are. Pay attention to the thoughts and beliefs that arise in your mind, particularly when faced with challenges or opportunities for growth. Notice any patterns of negative self-talk or self-doubt, and be mindful of how these beliefs impact your behavior and decisions. Common limiting beliefs include beliefs about our worthiness, capabilities, and potential for success. By shining a light on these beliefs, we can begin to challenge and transform them.

Questioning the evidence

Once you've identified a limiting belief, take a closer look at the evidence supporting it. Ask yourself: Is there any concrete evidence to support this belief, or is it based on assumptions or past experiences? Often, we hold onto limiting beliefs that are based on outdated information or distorted perceptions of reality. By questioning the evidence supporting these beliefs, we can begin to loosen their grip on our minds and open ourselves up to new possibilities.

Reframing negative thoughts

Another powerful strategy for challenging limiting beliefs is to reframe negative thoughts into more empowering and positive beliefs. Instead of focusing on what you can't do or why you're not good enough, reframe your thoughts to focus on what you can do and why you are worthy of success. For example, instead of thinking, "I'll never be successful," reframe it to, "I am capable of achieving my goals with hard work and determination." By consciously reframing negative thoughts, we can shift our perspective and create a more empowering mindset.

Seeking evidence to the contrary

Challenge your limiting beliefs by seeking evidence to the contrary. Look for examples of people who have overcome similar obstacles or achieved the goals you aspire to accomplish. Surround yourself with positive influences, whether it's books, podcasts, or role models who embody the beliefs and qualities you aspire to embody. By exposing yourself to evidence that contradicts your limiting beliefs, you'll weaken their hold on your mind and strengthen your belief in your ability to succeed.

Taking Action Despite Fear

Fear is a common driver of limiting beliefs, often holding us back from taking risks or pursuing our dreams. However, the only way to overcome fear is to take action despite it. Challenge yourself to step outside your comfort zone and take small, manageable steps towards your goals. Celebrate your successes and learn from your failures, knowing that each step forward brings you closer to breaking free from your limiting beliefs. By taking action despite fear, you'll build confidence, resilience, and a belief in your ability to overcome any obstacle.

Cultivating Self-Compassion

Finally, cultivate self-compassion as you work to overcome limiting beliefs. Recognize that challenging deeply ingrained beliefs takes time and patience, and be gentle with yourself along the way. Practice self-care, self-acceptance, and self-love, knowing that you are worthy and deserving of success and happiness. Treat yourself with the same kindness and compassion you would offer to a friend, and remember that you are capable of achieving anything you set your mind to.

Identifying and challenging limiting beliefs is a powerful step towards creating a life of abundance, success, and fulfillment. By recognizing these beliefs, questioning the evidence supporting them, reframing negative thoughts, seeking evidence to the contrary, taking action despite fear, and cultivating self-compassion, we can break free from their grip and unleash our full potential. Remember that you have the power to change your beliefs and create the life you desire; all it takes is the courage to challenge the limitations holding you back.

Practicing Positive Self-Talk and Affirmations

Positive self-talk and affirmations are powerful tools for cultivating a positive mindset, building self-confidence, and achieving your goals. They involve consciously directing your thoughts and words towards yourself in a supportive, uplifting, and encouraging manner. By replacing negative self-talk with positive affirmations, you can rewire your subconscious mind, boost your self-esteem, and create a more optimistic outlook on life.

Understanding positive self-talk

Positive self-talk is the practice of using supportive and empowering language when speaking to yourself. It involves replacing negative thoughts and beliefs with positive affirmations and encouraging statements. Instead of criticizing yourself or dwelling on your shortcomings, positive self-talk focuses on acknowledging your strengths, celebrating your accomplishments, and affirming your worth and potential. By consciously monitoring your internal dialogue and reframing negative thoughts in a positive light, you can cultivate a more resilient and empowered mindset.

Benefits of Positive Self-Talk

Practicing positive self-talk offers a multitude of benefits for your mental and emotional well-being. It helps to reduce stress and anxiety by promoting feelings of calmness and confidence. It enhances your self-esteem and self-confidence, enabling you to tackle challenges with greater resilience and determination. Positive self-talk also improves your overall mood and outlook on life, fostering a sense of optimism and gratitude. By cultivating a habit of positive self-talk, you'll create a more supportive and nurturing internal environment that empowers you to thrive in all areas of your life.

Introducing Affirmations

Affirmations are positive statements or phrases that affirm and reinforce desired beliefs, attitudes, and behaviors. They are typically short, concise, and written in the present tense, as if they are already true. Affirmations can be used to counteract negative self-talk, challenge limiting beliefs, and instill a sense of empowerment and confidence. Examples of affirmations include "I am capable of achieving my goals," "I am worthy of love and respect," and "I embrace challenges as opportunities for growth." By repeating affirmations regularly with conviction and belief, you can reprogram your subconscious mind and align your thoughts and actions with your desired outcomes.

How to Practice Positive Self-Talk and Affirmations

To practice positive self-talk and affirmations, start by becoming aware of your internal dialogue and identifying any negative or self-limiting beliefs that arise. Notice when you're being self-critical or doubting yourself, and consciously choose to replace those thoughts with positive affirmations. Write down a list of affirmations that resonate with you and reflect the qualities and traits you want to cultivate. Repeat these affirmations aloud or silently to yourself regularly, preferably in the morning or before bed when your mind is most receptive. Visualize yourself embodying the qualities and characteristics described in your affirmations, and feel the positive emotions associated with them. With consistent practice, you'll gradually rewire your brain to adopt more positive and empowering beliefs, leading to greater self-confidence and success.

Overcoming resistance and persistence

It's natural to encounter resistance when practicing positive self-talk and affirmations, especially if you've been accustomed to negative thinking patterns for a long time. You may find yourself doubting the effectiveness of affirmations or feeling uncomfortable repeating positive statements about yourself. It's important to persist despite these challenges and trust in the process. Remember that change takes time and consistency, and be patient with yourself as you work to shift your mindset. Surround yourself with supportive influences, such as uplifting books, affirming podcasts, or like-minded individuals who can encourage and inspire you on your journey.

Practicing positive self-talk and affirmations is a powerful way to cultivate a more optimistic, confident, and empowered mindset. By consciously directing your thoughts and words towards yourself in a supportive and uplifting manner, you can rewire your subconscious mind, boost your self-esteem, and align your thoughts and actions with your desired outcomes.

Make positive self-talk and affirmations a regular part of your daily routine, and watch as they transform your mindset and your life for the better.

Cultivating Resilience in the Face of Setbacks

Resilience is the ability to bounce back from adversity, overcome challenges, and thrive in the face of setbacks. It's a quality that can be cultivated and strengthened through practice and perseverance. In today's unpredictable world, cultivating resilience is more important than ever, as it enables us to navigate life's ups and downs with grace and resilience.

<u>Here are some strategies for cultivating resilience in the face of setbacks:</u>

- Embrace Change and Uncertainty: Change is inevitable, and uncertainty is a constant part of life. Instead of resisting change or fearing the unknown, embrace it as an opportunity for growth and adaptation. Cultivate a mindset of flexibility and openness, and trust in your ability to navigate whatever challenges come your way.
- Develop a Growth Mindset: A growth mindset is the belief that challenges are opportunities for learning and growth. Instead of viewing setbacks as failures, see them as valuable lessons that can help you grow stronger and more resilient. Focus on what you can control, and approach setbacks with curiosity, optimism, and a willingness to learn.
- Practice self-compassion: When faced with setbacks, it's important to be kind and compassionate towards yourself. Avoid self-criticism or blame, and instead

offer yourself the same kindness and support you would give to a friend in need. Remember that setbacks are a natural part of life, and they do not define your worth or capabilities.

- Build a Support Network: Surround yourself with supportive friends, family members, and mentors who can offer encouragement, guidance, and perspective during difficult times. Lean on your support network for emotional support, practical help, and a listening ear when you need it most. Connecting with others who have faced similar challenges can also provide validation and reassurance that you're not alone.

- Focus on Solutions: Instead of dwelling on the problem, focus your energy on finding solutions and taking proactive steps towards overcoming setbacks. Break down big challenges into smaller, more manageable steps, and tackle them one at a time. Celebrate your progress along the way, no matter how small, and maintain a sense of optimism and determination as you work towards your goals.

- Practice Mindfulness and Self-Care: Mindfulness practices, such as meditation, deep breathing, or yoga, can help calm the mind, reduce stress, and build emotional resilience. Make self-care a priority by prioritizing activities that nourish your body, mind, and spirit, such as exercise, healthy eating, spending time in nature, or pursuing hobbies and interests that bring you joy.

- Cultivate Gratitude and Optimism: Cultivating an attitude of gratitude and optimism can help shift your perspective and build resilience in the face of setbacks. Focus on the positive aspects of your life, no matter how small, and practice gratitude daily for the blessings you have. Maintain a hopeful outlook for the future, and remind yourself that setbacks are temporary and opportunities for growth and transformation exist.

Cultivating resilience in the face of setbacks is essential for navigating life's challenges with grace and resilience. By embracing change and uncertainty, developing a growth mindset, practicing self-compassion, building a support network, focusing on solutions, practicing mindfulness and self-care, and cultivating gratitude and optimism, you can strengthen your resilience and thrive in the face of adversity. Remember that setbacks are not the end of the road but rather opportunities for growth, learning, and personal transformation.

Adopting a Growth Mindset for Continuous Improvement

A growth mindset is the belief that our abilities and intelligence can be developed through dedication, effort, and learning. This mindset contrasts with a fixed mindset, which sees qualities like intelligence and talent as innate and unchangeable. Adopting a growth mindset is essential for continuous improvement and personal development.

<u>Here's how to cultivate a growth mindset:</u>

- Embrace Challenges: Instead of avoiding challenges, see them as opportunities for growth and learning.

Approach new tasks and experiences with curiosity and enthusiasm, knowing that they will help you develop new skills and abilities.

- Learn from Failure: Failure is a natural part of the learning process. Instead of viewing failure as a sign of inadequacy, see it as a valuable learning opportunity. Reflect on what went wrong, identify lessons learned, and use that knowledge to improve and grow.

- Cultivate Persistence: Developing a growth mindset requires persistence and resilience. Stay committed to your goals, even when faced with obstacles or setbacks. Persevere through challenges, knowing that your efforts will eventually lead to progress and success.

- Value Effort and Hard Work: In a growth mindset, effort and hard work are valued more than natural talent or ability. Recognize the importance of putting in consistent effort and pushing yourself outside your comfort zone to achieve your goals.

- Seek feedback and criticism. Feedback is essential for growth and improvement. Welcome constructive criticism as an opportunity to learn and grow, and use feedback to identify areas for development and refinement.

- Focus on the Process: Instead of solely focusing on outcomes or results, pay attention to the process of learning and growth. Celebrate your progress, no matter how small, and acknowledge the effort and dedication you've put in to reach your goals.

- Cultivate a Love for Learning: Adopt a lifelong attitude of curiosity and a love for learning. Seek out new experiences, explore different interests, and continuously challenge yourself to expand your knowledge and skills.
- Surround yourself with growth-minded individuals. Surround yourself with people who embody a growth mindset and who inspire and support your journey of continuous improvement. Learn from their experiences, seek their guidance and encouragement, and collaborate with them to achieve common goals.

By adopting a growth mindset, you can unlock your full potential, overcome obstacles, and achieve continuous improvement in all areas of your life. Cultivate a mindset of resilience, persistence, and a love for learning, and embrace challenges as opportunities for growth and development. With dedication, effort, and a commitment to lifelong learning, you can achieve your goals and create a life of fulfillment and success.

Visualizing Success and Manifesting Your Goals

Visualizing success and manifesting your goals involves harnessing the power of your imagination to create a clear and vivid mental image of the outcomes you desire. By consistently visualizing yourself achieving your goals and embodying the success you wish to attain, you can program your subconscious mind to work towards making those visions a reality.

Visualization is a technique used by athletes, performers, and successful individuals across various fields to enhance performance, increase motivation, and overcome obstacles. When you visualize success, you activate the same neural pathways in your brain that are activated when you actually experience that success, reinforcing positive beliefs and attitudes that support your goals.

To begin visualizing success and manifesting your goals, find a quiet and comfortable space where you won't be disturbed. Close your eyes and take a few deep breaths to relax your body and clear your mind. Then, start to visualize yourself achieving your goals in vivid detail.

Imagine yourself in the future, having already accomplished your goals. See yourself enjoying the fruits of your labor, experiencing the emotions of success, and celebrating your achievements. Visualize the specific outcomes you desire, such as landing your dream job, achieving financial abundance, or reaching a personal milestone.

Engage all your senses in the visualization process. Imagine what you would see, hear, feel, and even taste and smell in this moment of success. Visualize yourself interacting with others, receiving recognition and praise, and feeling a sense of fulfillment and satisfaction.

As you visualize success, focus on the positive emotions associated with achieving your goals. Feel the excitement, joy, and gratitude that come with realizing your dreams. Allow yourself to fully immerse yourself in these feelings, as if they were already true in the present moment.

Repeat this visualization exercise regularly, ideally on a daily basis. The more vividly and consistently you visualize your goals, the more deeply ingrained they become in your subconscious mind. Over time, your subconscious will work tirelessly to align your thoughts, beliefs, and actions with the outcomes you desire, making them more likely to manifest in your reality.

In addition to visualization, you can enhance the manifestation of your goals by taking inspired action towards them. Use the clarity and motivation gained from visualization to set specific, achievable goals and create a plan of action to achieve them. Break down your goals into smaller, manageable steps, and take consistent action towards them each day.

Stay open to opportunities and remain flexible in your approach, knowing that the path to success may not always be linear. Trust in the process and believe in your ability to achieve your goals, even in the face of obstacles or setbacks. By combining the power of visualization with focused action and a positive mindset, you can manifest your goals and create the life you desire.

Chapter 3:
Cultivate Positivity

Gratitude Practices for Daily Life

Practicing gratitude is a simple yet powerful way to cultivate a positive mindset, enhance your well-being, and improve your overall quality of life. By consciously focusing on the things you're thankful for, you can shift your perspective from what's lacking to what's abundant and create a greater sense of joy, fulfillment, and contentment in your daily life.

One of the most effective gratitude practices is keeping a gratitude journal. Take a few minutes each day to write down three things you're grateful for. These could be big things, like achieving a milestone or receiving a promotion, or small things, like a beautiful sunset or a kind gesture from a friend. Reflect on why you're grateful for each item and allow yourself to fully experience the feelings of appreciation and abundance.

Another practice of gratitude is expressing gratitude to others. Take time to thank the people in your life who have made a positive impact on you, whether it's a family member, friend, colleague, or even a stranger. Send a heartfelt thank-you note, make a phone call, or simply express your gratitude in person. Not only will this strengthen your relationships and deepen your connections with others, but it will also reinforce your own feelings of gratitude and appreciation.

Practicing gratitude doesn't have to be limited to specific activities; you can incorporate gratitude into your daily routine in various ways. Start your day by expressing gratitude for the opportunities and blessings that await you. Throughout the day, pause to notice and appreciate the beauty and abundance that surrounds you, whether it's the warmth of the sun on your face or the sound of laughter in the air. Before bed, take a moment to reflect on the day and give thanks for the experiences, lessons, and moments of joy it brought.

In addition to these practices, you can cultivate a mindset of gratitude by shifting your focus from what you don't have to what you do have. Instead of dwelling on what's missing or lacking in your life, focus on the abundance and blessings that exist all around you. Challenge yourself to find something to be grateful for in every situation, even in difficult or challenging times. By choosing to see the good in every situation, you can train your mind to default to a state of gratitude and appreciation.

As you incorporate gratitude practices into your daily life, you'll begin to notice profound changes in your mindset and outlook. You'll feel more optimistic, resilient, and at peace with yourself and the world around you. By cultivating an attitude of gratitude, you'll invite more joy, abundance, and fulfillment into your life, creating a positive ripple effect that extends to every aspect of your being.

Keeping a Gratitude Journal

Keeping a gratitude journal is a simple yet powerful practice that can have profound effects on your well-being and overall happiness. It involves regularly writing down the things you're thankful for, whether big or small, and reflecting on the blessings and abundance in your life.

To start a gratitude journal, all you need is a notebook or a digital document where you can record your thoughts and reflections. Set aside a few minutes each day to write down three things you're grateful for. These could be anything from meaningful relationships and personal achievements to simple pleasures like a delicious meal or a beautiful sunset.

As you write in your gratitude journal, take the time to reflect on why you're grateful for each item. Notice how it makes you feel and the impact it has on your mood and outlook. Allow yourself to fully experience the feelings of appreciation and abundance that arise as you express gratitude for the blessings in your life.

It's important to be consistent with your gratitude practice, so try to make it a daily habit. Choose a time that works best for you, whether it's first thing in the morning, before bed, or during a quiet moment in your day. Incorporate your gratitude journaling into your routine to ensure that it becomes a regular part of your life.

The beauty of keeping a gratitude journal is that it trains your mind to focus on the positive aspects of your life, even during challenging times. By consciously directing your attention towards what's going well and what you're thankful for, you can shift your perspective from scarcity to abundance and cultivate a greater sense of joy and contentment.

Over time, you may begin to notice profound changes in your mindset and outlook. You'll feel more optimistic, resilient, and appreciative of the blessings in your life. Keeping a gratitude journal can also help reduce stress, anxiety, and depression, as it encourages you to focus on the present moment and the things you have to be thankful for.

In addition to the mental and emotional benefits, keeping a gratitude journal can also strengthen your relationships and deepen your connections with others. Expressing gratitude to the people in your life can foster a sense of appreciation and goodwill, leading to stronger bonds and a greater sense of community.

Keeping a gratitude journal is a simple yet transformative practice that can enhance your well-being and enrich your life in countless ways. By regularly acknowledging and appreciating the blessings in your life, you can cultivate a mindset of gratitude and abundance that will positively impact every aspect of your being. So grab a pen and paper, or open a new document on your computer, and start jotting down the things you're grateful for today. Your future self will thank you.

Surrounding Yourself with Positive Influences

Surrounding yourself with positive influences is essential for maintaining a healthy mindset and achieving your goals. The people you spend time with, the media you consume, and the environment you inhabit all have a significant impact on your thoughts, feelings, and behaviors. By intentionally surrounding yourself with positivity, you can enhance your well-being, boost your motivation, and create a more supportive and uplifting environment for personal growth and success.

One of the most important aspects of surrounding yourself with positive influences is choosing the right people to spend time with. Surround yourself with individuals who inspire and uplift you, who share your values and goals, and who support your personal and professional development. Seek out friends, family members, mentors, and colleagues who encourage you to be your best self and who believe in your potential.

It's also important to be mindful of the media you consume and the content you expose yourself to on a daily basis. Limit your exposure to negative news, gossip, and social media, which can drain your energy and lower your mood. Instead, seek out sources of inspiration, motivation, and positivity, such as uplifting books, podcasts, and online communities that align with your interests and values.

Creating a positive physical environment is another key aspect of surrounding yourself with positive influences. Surround yourself with objects, colors, and decorations that evoke feelings of joy, peace, and inspiration. Declutter your space and organize it in a way that promotes relaxation and productivity. Spend time in nature whenever possible, as being outdoors can have a rejuvenating and uplifting effect on your mood and mindset.

In addition to your external environment, it's important to cultivate a positive internal dialogue and mindset. Practice self-care activities that nourish your body, mind, and spirit, such as exercise, meditation, and creative expression. Develop a gratitude practice to focus on the blessings and abundance in your life, and challenge negative thoughts and beliefs with positive affirmations and reframing techniques.

Finally, remember that you have the power to choose the influences that surround you and the impact they have on your life. Be intentional about who and what you allow into your inner circle, and don't be afraid to distance yourself from negative influences that hold you back or drag you down. Surround yourself with positivity, and watch as it transforms your mindset, your relationships, and your life for the better.

Letting Go of Negativity and Resentment

Letting go of negativity and resentment is essential for living a fulfilling and peaceful life. Holding onto negative emotions can weigh us down, drain our energy, and prevent us from experiencing true happiness and inner peace. By releasing negativity and resentment, we can free ourselves from the past and create space for positivity, joy, and growth in our lives.

One of the first steps in letting go of negativity and resentment is acknowledging and accepting the emotions we're experiencing. Allow yourself to feel whatever emotions arise without judgment or resistance. Recognize that it's normal to feel anger, sadness, or frustration at times, but holding onto these emotions indefinitely can be harmful to our mental and emotional well-being.

Once you've acknowledged your emotions, it's important to take responsibility for them and take proactive steps to address them. Identify the source of your negativity and resentment, whether it's a past experience, a current situation, or a relationship. Reflect on how holding onto these emotions is impacting your life and your relationships, and consider the toll it's taking on your mental and emotional health.

Next, practice forgiveness and compassion towards yourself and others. Forgiveness doesn't mean condoning or excusing the behavior that hurt you, but rather releasing the hold it has over your life. Recognize that holding onto resentment only harms you in the long run, and choose to let go of the past and move forward with an open heart and mind.

Another helpful practice for letting go of negativity and resentment is gratitude. Cultivate a mindset of gratitude by focusing on the blessings and abundance in your life rather than dwelling on what's lacking or missing. Practice gratitude daily by counting your blessings, keeping a gratitude journal, or simply pausing to appreciate the beauty and goodness around you.

In addition to forgiveness and gratitude, practice self-care activities that nurture your body, mind, and spirit. Engage in activities that bring you joy and relaxation, such as spending time in nature, practicing yoga or meditation, or pursuing hobbies and interests that energize you. Take care of your physical health by eating nutritious foods, getting regular exercise, and getting enough rest and sleep.

Finally, surround yourself with positive influences and supportive people who uplift and encourage you on your journey towards letting go of negativity and resentment. Seek out friends, family members, or a therapist who can provide support and guidance as you navigate your emotions and work towards healing and transformation.

Remember that letting go of negativity and resentment is a process that takes time and practice. Be patient with yourself, and celebrate your progress along the way. By releasing the past and embracing the present moment with an open heart and mind, you can create a life filled with joy, peace, and fulfillment.

Finding Silver Linings in Challenges

Life is full of challenges, obstacles, and setbacks. Whether it's a personal hardship, a professional setback, or a global crisis, facing difficult situations is an inevitable part of the human experience. While it's natural to feel overwhelmed, frustrated, or discouraged when encountering challenges, it's also possible to find silver linings—hidden blessings or opportunities for growth—even in the most difficult circumstances.

One of the first steps in finding silver linings in challenges is shifting your perspective. Instead of viewing challenges as insurmountable obstacles or sources of despair, try to see them as opportunities for growth, learning, and personal development. Recognize that facing challenges can build resilience, strength, and character, and that overcoming obstacles can ultimately lead to greater success and fulfillment in the long run.

Another helpful approach is reframing negative situations in a more positive light. Look for potential benefits or opportunities that may arise from the challenge you're facing. Ask yourself questions like, What can I learn from this experience? How can I grow stronger as a result of overcoming this obstacle? What unexpected blessings or opportunities might emerge from this difficulty?

Practicing gratitude can also help you find silver linings in challenges. Take time each day to focus on the things you're thankful for, even amidst difficult circumstances. Reflect on the lessons, blessings, or moments of grace that have emerged from the challenges you've faced. By cultivating an attitude of gratitude, you can shift your focus from what's lacking to what's abundant, even in the midst of adversity.

Seeking support from others can also help you find silver linings in challenges. Surround yourself with positive, supportive people who can offer encouragement, guidance, and perspective during difficult times. Share your challenges openly and honestly with trusted friends, family members, or mentors, and allow them to support you on your journey towards finding silver linings and overcoming obstacles.

Finally, practice self-care and resilience-building activities that nurture your physical, mental, and emotional well-being. Engage in activities that bring you joy, relaxation, and a sense of purpose, such as spending time in nature, practicing mindfulness or meditation, or pursuing hobbies and interests that energize you. Take care of your physical health by eating nutritious foods, getting regular exercise, and getting enough rest and sleep.

Finding silver linings in challenges is a powerful mindset shift that can help you navigate difficult times with grace, resilience, and optimism. By shifting your perspective, reframing negative situations, practicing gratitude, seeking support from others, and prioritizing self-care, you can uncover hidden blessings and opportunities for growth even in the midst of adversity. Remember that challenges are not obstacles to your happiness and success but rather opportunities for growth, learning, and personal transformation.

Spreading Kindness and Compassion to Others

Kindness and compassion are powerful forces for good in the world. By spreading kindness and compassion to others, we not only make a positive impact on their lives but also contribute to creating a more caring, supportive, and harmonious society.

Here are some ways to spread kindness and compassion to others:

- Show Empathy: Put yourself in others' shoes and try to understand their perspectives, feelings, and experiences. Listen actively and attentively when others share their struggles or challenges, and offer empathy and support without judgment or criticism.

- Practice Random Acts of Kindness: Perform small acts of kindness and generosity for others without expecting anything in return. This could be as simple as holding the door open for someone, paying for a stranger's coffee, or leaving a kind note for a friend or colleague.

- Offer Support: Be there for others in their time of need, offering practical help, emotional support, or a listening ear. Reach out to friends, family members, or acquaintances who may be going through a difficult time, and let them know you're there to support them in any way you can.

- Volunteer Your Time: Dedicate your time and energy to volunteering for causes and organizations that are meaningful to you. Whether it's serving meals at a homeless shelter, tutoring children in need, or participating in environmental clean-up efforts, volunteering allows you to make a tangible difference in the lives of others and contribute to the greater good.

- Practice Forgiveness: Let go of grudges, resentments, and judgments towards others, and practice forgiveness and understanding instead. Recognize that everyone makes mistakes and deserves compassion and second chances. By forgiving others, you free yourself from the burden of carrying negative emotions and open the door to healing and reconciliation.

- Spread Positivity: Be a source of positivity and encouragement to those around you. Offer words of encouragement, praise, and appreciation to friends, family members, colleagues, and even strangers. Share uplifting stories, quotes, and experiences that inspire and uplift others.

- Be Kind to Yourself: Remember that spreading kindness and compassion to others starts with being kind to yourself. Treat yourself with the same love, care, and compassion that you extend to others. Practice self-care activities that nourish your body, mind, and spirit, and cultivate a mindset of self-compassion and acceptance.

- Lead by example: Be a role model for kindness and compassion in your community and beyond. Lead by example in your words, actions, and interactions with others, demonstrating empathy, generosity, and understanding in all your relationships and encounters.

Spreading kindness and compassion to others is a simple yet powerful way to make a positive impact on the world and foster a culture of caring and compassion. By practicing empathy, performing random acts of kindness, offering support, volunteering your time, practicing forgiveness, spreading positivity, being kind to yourself, and leading by example, you can contribute to creating a world where kindness and compassion are valued and celebrated. Remember that even small acts of kindness can have a ripple effect, touching the lives of countless others and creating a more compassionate and connected world for all.

Chapter 4:
Journey of Reflection

Reflecting on Past Achievements and Failures

Reflecting on past achievements and failures is an important practice for personal growth and development. It allows us to gain insights, learn valuable lessons, and make informed decisions about our future endeavors. Whether we've experienced success or setbacks, taking the time to reflect on our past experiences can provide valuable perspective and help us move forward with greater clarity and purpose.

When reflecting on past achievements, it's important to celebrate our successes and acknowledge the hard work, dedication, and perseverance that led to their attainment. Take pride in your accomplishments, no matter how big or small, and recognize the strengths, skills, and qualities that contributed to your success. Reflect on the challenges you overcame, the lessons you learned, and the growth you experienced along the way. Use your past achievements as a source of motivation and inspiration for future endeavors, knowing that you have the ability to overcome obstacles and achieve your goals.

Similarly, reflecting on past failures can provide valuable insights and opportunities for growth. Instead of dwelling on past mistakes or shortcomings, approach failure as a learning experience and an opportunity for self-improvement. Ask yourself what went wrong, what you could have done differently, and what lessons you can take away from the experience. Embrace failure as a natural part of the learning process and a stepping stone to future success. Use your past failures as a catalyst for growth and resilience, knowing that each setback brings you one step closer to your goals.

In addition to reflecting on individual achievements and failures, it can also be helpful to examine patterns and trends in your past experiences. Identify recurring themes, behaviors, or habits that have contributed to your success or hindered your progress. Reflect on what has worked well for you in the past and what areas may require improvement or adjustment. Use this insight to set goals, develop action plans, and make informed decisions about your future endeavors.

Finally, remember that reflection is an ongoing process that requires time, patience, and self-awareness. Make reflection a regular practice in your life, setting aside time to review your past experiences, assess your progress, and plan for the future. Cultivate a mindset of curiosity, openness, and growth, and approach each reflection with a spirit of inquiry and exploration.

Reflecting on past achievements and failures is a valuable practice for personal growth and development. By celebrating our successes, learning from our failures, and examining patterns in our past experiences, we can gain valuable insights, make informed decisions, and move forward with greater clarity, purpose, and resilience. Embrace reflection as a tool for self-discovery and empowerment, knowing that each reflection brings you one step closer to becoming the best version of yourself.

Clarifying Your Values and Priorities

Clarifying your values and priorities is essential for living a meaningful and purposeful life. Your values are the principles, beliefs, and ideals that guide your behavior and decision-making, while your priorities are the things that matter most to you and deserve your time, attention, and energy. By clarifying your values and priorities, you can align your actions with what truly matters to you and create a life that reflects your authentic self.

One of the first steps in clarifying your values and priorities is self-reflection. Take the time to reflect on what is most important to you in life—what brings you joy, fulfillment, and a sense of purpose. Think about the principles and beliefs that you hold dear, and consider how they influence your thoughts, actions, and relationships. Ask yourself questions like: What do I value most in life? What kind of person do I want to be? What legacy do I want to leave behind?

Once you've identified your values, prioritize them based on their importance to you. Consider which values are non-negotiable and which ones may require more attention or development. Be honest with yourself about what truly matters to you, even if it means making difficult choices or sacrifices. Remember that clarifying your priorities is about making intentional decisions that align with your values and support your overall well-being and happiness.

It can also be helpful to identify your long-term goals and aspirations when clarifying your values and priorities. Think about what you want to achieve in different areas of your life, such as career, relationships, health, and personal growth, and consider how your values and priorities can guide you towards these goals. Use your values and priorities as a compass to navigate the decisions and choices you make on a daily basis, ensuring that they are in alignment with your long-term vision for yourself and your life.

In addition to self-reflection, seek feedback from trusted friends, family members, or mentors who know you well and can provide valuable insights into your values and priorities. Listen to their perspectives and observations with an open mind, and consider how their feedback aligns with your own self-awareness and understanding.

Finally, remember that clarifying your values and priorities is an ongoing process that may evolve over time as you grow and change. Stay open to new experiences, perspectives, and opportunities that may challenge or expand your understanding of yourself and what matters most to you. Revisit and revise your values and priorities regularly to ensure they remain aligned with your evolving goals and aspirations.

Clarifying your values and priorities is a powerful practice that can help you live a more meaningful, purposeful, and fulfilling life. By taking the time to reflect on what truly matters to you, prioritizing your values, setting goals that align with your priorities, seeking feedback from others, and remaining open to growth and change, you can create a life that reflects your authentic self and brings you joy, fulfillment, and a sense of purpose.

Identifying What Truly Matters to You

Identifying what truly matters to you is an important step towards living a fulfilling and authentic life. It involves gaining clarity on your values, priorities, and aspirations and aligning your actions with what brings you joy, fulfillment, and meaning. By understanding what truly matters to you, you can make more intentional decisions, set meaningful goals, and create a life that reflects your authentic self.

One approach to identifying what truly matters to you is self-reflection. Take the time to reflect on your experiences, beliefs, and emotions to gain insight into your values and priorities. Consider what brings you the greatest sense of joy, fulfillment, and purpose in life. Think about the activities, relationships, and experiences that energize you and make you feel alive. Ask yourself questions like: What activities do I enjoy doing in my free time? What values do I hold dear? What goals do I want to achieve in life?

Another approach is to pay attention to your emotions and intuition. Notice how you feel in different situations and environments, and pay attention to the emotions that arise when you're engaging in certain activities or spending time with certain people. Your emotions can provide valuable clues about what truly matters to you and what brings you the greatest sense of satisfaction and fulfillment.

It can also be helpful to examine your past experiences and accomplishments to gain insight into your values and priorities. Look back on moments of success, happiness, and fulfillment in your life and identify the underlying values and priorities that were present during those times. Consider the goals you've achieved and the experiences that have brought you the most joy and fulfillment. Reflect on what those experiences have taught you about yourself and what truly matters to you.

In addition to self-reflection, seek feedback from trusted friends, family members, or mentors who know you well and can provide insight into your values and priorities. Listen to their perspectives and observations with an open mind, and consider how their feedback aligns with your own self-awareness and understanding.

As you identify what truly matters to you, remember that your values and priorities may evolve over time as you grow and change. Stay open to new experiences, perspectives, and opportunities that may challenge or expand your understanding of yourself and what matters most to you. Be willing to adjust your goals and priorities as needed to ensure they remain aligned with your authentic self and your vision for a fulfilling life.

Identifying what truly matters to you is a deeply personal and introspective process that requires self-awareness, reflection, and honesty. By taking the time to understand your values, priorities, and aspirations, you can create a life that reflects your authentic self and brings you joy, fulfillment, and meaning. Trust yourself and your intuition, and be willing to explore and embrace what truly matters to you, knowing that it is the key to living a life of purpose and fulfillment.

Exploring Your Passions and Interests

Reflect on your past experiences:

- Think about activities or hobbies that you've enjoyed in the past.
- Consider any subjects or topics that have sparked your curiosity or enthusiasm.
- Reflect on moments when you've felt the most fulfilled or engaged in what you were doing.

Try new things:

- Be open to exploring new activities, hobbies, or interests.
- Take classes or workshops in subjects that intrigue you.
- Volunteer for different organizations or causes to discover new passions.

Pay Attention to Your Emotions:

- Notice how you feel when you're engaged in different activities.
- Pay attention to the activities or topics that make you feel excited, energized, or fulfilled.
- Trust your intuition and follow your gut instincts when exploring new interests.

Seek Inspiration:

- Read books, watch documentaries, or listen to podcasts on subjects that interest you.
- Surround yourself with people who are passionate about their interests and hobbies.

- Attend events, conferences, or seminars related to topics that intrigue you.

Experiment and iterate:
- Don't be afraid to experiment and try different things.
- Give yourself permission to explore multiple interests and see what resonates with you.
- Be open to the possibility that your passions and interests may evolve over time.

Reflect and evaluate:
- Regularly reflect on your experiences and evaluate what brings you the most joy and fulfillment.
- Consider how your passions and interests align with your values, goals, and aspirations.
- Continuously refine and adjust your pursuits based on what brings you the greatest sense of satisfaction and meaning.

Stay curious and open-minded.
- Cultivate a mindset of curiosity and openness to new experiences.
- Embrace uncertainty and be willing to explore unfamiliar territory.
- Keep an open mind and be receptive to discovering new passions and interests along the way.

Exploring your passions and interests is a journey of self-discovery and personal growth. By reflecting on your past experiences, trying new things, paying attention to your emotions, seeking inspiration, experimenting and iterating, reflecting and evaluating, and staying curious and open-minded, you can uncover new passions and interests that bring joy, fulfillment, and meaning to your life.

Reconnecting with Your Inner Child and Authentic Self

Reconnecting with your inner child and authentic self is a powerful journey of self-discovery and personal growth. It involves revisiting the innocence, curiosity, and joy of childhood and reconnecting with the true essence of who you are. By embracing your inner child and honoring your authentic self, you can cultivate greater self-awareness, acceptance, and fulfillment in your life.

One way to reconnect with your inner child is to engage in activities that bring you joy and spontaneity. Allow yourself to play, explore, and have fun like you did as a child. Rediscover hobbies, interests, and activities that once brought you happiness, whether it's painting, dancing, singing, or simply spending time in nature. Embrace the sense of wonder and curiosity that comes with exploring the world around you, and allow yourself to experience life with a childlike sense of wonder.

Another way to reconnect with your inner child is to practice self-compassion and acceptance. Treat yourself with the same kindness, love, and understanding that you would offer a child. Be gentle with yourself and acknowledge your imperfections and vulnerabilities without judgment or criticism. Allow yourself to feel and express your emotions authentically, knowing that it's okay to experience a full range of feelings, just as a child does.

In addition to embracing your inner child, reconnecting with your authentic self involves getting in touch with your core values, beliefs, and desires. Take the time to reflect on what truly matters to you and what brings you a sense of purpose and meaning in life. Identify the values and principles that guide your decisions and actions, and strive to live in alignment with them. Trust your intuition and inner wisdom to lead you towards paths that are authentic and fulfilling for you.

Practice self-expression and creativity as a means of connecting with your authentic self. Allow yourself to express your thoughts, feelings, and ideas freely through writing, art, music, or other creative outlets. Use creativity as a tool for self-discovery and self-expression, allowing it to illuminate the unique essence of who you are.

Finally, surround yourself with people who accept and appreciate you for who you truly are. Seek out relationships and connections that nurture and support your authentic self-expression and growth. Surround yourself with individuals who encourage you to embrace your uniqueness, celebrate your strengths, and express yourself authentically without fear of judgment or rejection.

Reconnecting with your inner child and authentic self is a journey of self-discovery, acceptance, and growth. By embracing the innocence, curiosity, and joy of childhood, practicing self-compassion and acceptance, getting in touch with your core values and desires, expressing yourself creatively, and surrounding yourself with supportive relationships, you can cultivate a deeper sense of self-awareness, fulfillment, and authenticity in your life. Remember that your inner child is always within you, waiting to be rediscovered and embraced as an integral part of who you are.

Setting Intentions for Future Growth and Development

Setting intentions for future growth and development is a proactive and empowering practice that allows you to clarify your goals, focus your energy, and create a roadmap for personal and professional advancement. By setting clear intentions, you can align your actions with your aspirations and take deliberate steps towards realizing your full potential.

Here are some straightforward steps to guide you in setting intentions for future growth anddevelopment:

Reflect on your values and priorities:
- Take time to reflect on what truly matters to you in life.
- Identify your core values, beliefs, and priorities that guide your decisions and actions.
- Consider what areas of your life you want to focus on for growth and development, whether it's career advancement, personal relationships, health and wellness, or personal growth.

Clarify your goals and aspirations:
- Define specific, measurable, and achievable goals that align with your values and priorities.

- Break down your long-term goals into smaller, manageable milestones or action steps.
- Consider both short-term and long-term goals that contribute to your overall growth and development.

Visualize Your Ideal Future:

- Take time to visualize what your ideal future looks like in different areas of your life.
- Use visualization techniques to imagine yourself achieving your goals and living the life you desire.
- Allow yourself to feel the emotions associated with accomplishing your intentions, such as joy, fulfillment, and success.

Set clear intentions:

- Write down your intentions in clear, affirmative language.
- Be specific about what you want to achieve and why it's important to you.
- Use present--tense statements to affirm your intentions as if they have already been accomplished.

Create an action plan:

- Develop a detailed action plan outlining the steps you need to take to achieve your intentions.
- Break down each intention into actionable tasks and deadlines.

- Identify any potential obstacles or challenges, challenges, and brainstorm strategies to overcome them.

Stay committed and flexible.

- Commit to taking consistent action towards your intentions, even when faced with setbacks or obstacles.
- Stay flexible and open to adjusting your plans as needed based on feedback and new information.
- Practice self-discipline and resilience to stay focused and motivated on your path to growth and development.

Review and adjust regularly.

- Regularly review your progress towards your intentions and celebrate your successes along the way.
- Reflect on what's working well and what areas may need adjustment or refinement.
- Stay committed to your growth and development journey, and be willing to adapt and evolve as you progress.

Setting intentions for future growth and development is a proactive and empowering practice that allows you to clarify your goals, focus your energy, and create a roadmap for personal and professional advancement. By reflecting on your values and priorities, clarifying your goals and aspirations, visualizing your ideal future, setting clear intentions, creating an action plan, staying committed and flexible, and regularly reviewing and adjusting your plans, you can set yourself up for success and create a life that aligns with your deepest desires and aspirations.

Chapter 5:
The Rhythm of Routine

Establishing a Morning Routine for Success

Establishing a morning routine for success is a powerful way to set the tone for your day, boost your productivity, and enhance your overall well-being. A well-designed morning routine can help you start your day on the right foot, increase your energy levels, and cultivate habits that contribute to your success and happiness. Here are some straightforward steps to help you establish a morning routine for success:

Wake up early:

- Set your alarm for an early wake-up time that allows you to have ample time for your morning routine.
- Aim to wake up at the same time each day to establish a consistent sleep schedule and optimize your body's natural circadian rhythm.

Hydrate Your Body:

- Start your morning by drinking a glass of water to rehydrate your body after a night of sleep.
- Hydrating your body first thing in the morning helps jumpstart your metabolism, boost your energy levels, and improve your overall well-being.

Practice mindfulness or meditation.
- Take a few minutes to practice mindfulness or meditation to center your mind and set a positive intention for the day.
- Focus on your breath, body sensations, or guided meditation to cultivate a sense of calm and clarity before starting your day.

Move your body:
- Incorporate some form of physical activity into your morning routine, such as stretching, yoga, or a quick workout.
- Moving your body in the morning helps increase blood flow, boost energy levels, and improve mood and cognitive function.

Nourish Your Body:
- Enjoy a nutritious breakfast that fuels your body and provides sustained energy throughout the morning.
- Choose foods that are rich in protein, fiber, and healthy fats to keep you feeling full and satisfied until your next meal.

Set daily goals:
- Take a few moments to review your goals for the day and prioritize your tasks and activities.
- Write down your top priorities for the day and create a plan for how you will accomplish them.

Practice Gratitude:

- Take time to reflect on what you're grateful for and express gratitude for the blessings in your life.
- Cultivating an attitude of gratitude helps shift your mindset towards positivity and abundance, setting the stage for a successful and fulfilling day.

Limit Distractions:

- Minimize distractions during your morning routine by avoiding checking email, social media, or news first thing in the morning.
- Create a peaceful and focused environment by turning off notifications and setting boundaries with technology.

Engage in personal growth activities:

- Dedicate time to engage in activities that promote personal growth and development, such as reading, journaling, or learning something new.
- Invest in yourself and prioritize activities that nourish your mind, body, and spirit.

Practice Consistency:

- Consistency is key to establishing a successful morning routine. Stick to your routine even on weekends or days when you feel less motivated.
- Over time, your morning routine will become a habit, making it easier to maintain and reap the benefits of a successful start to your day.

Establishing a morning routine for success is a simple yet powerful way to optimize your mornings and set yourself up for a productive, fulfilling, and successful day ahead. By incorporating activities such as waking up early, hydrating your body, practicing mindfulness or meditation, moving your body, nourishing your body with a nutritious breakfast, setting daily goals, practicing gratitude, limiting distractions, engaging in personal growth activities, and practicing consistency, you can create a morning routine that supports your overall well-being and helps you achieve your goals and aspirations.

Incorporating Exercise and Movement into Your Daily Life

Incorporating exercise and movement into your daily life is essential for maintaining physical health, improving mental well-being, and enhancing your overall quality of life. By making regular physical activity a priority, you can experience numerous benefits, including increased energy levels, reduced stress, improved mood, and better physical fitness. Here are some straightforward ways to incorporate exercise and movement into your daily routine:

Schedule regular workouts:

- Set aside dedicated time in your daily schedule for exercise, whether it's in the morning, during your lunch break, or in the evening.
- Choose activities that you enjoy and that fit your fitness level and preferences, such as walking, jogging, cycling, swimming, or group fitness classes.

Stay Active Throughout the Day:
- Look for opportunities to incorporate movement into your daily activities, such as taking the stairs instead of the elevator, walking or biking to work, or doing household chores like cleaning or gardening.
- Break up long periods of sitting with short bursts of activity, such as stretching or walking around your office every hour.

Make It Social:
- Exercise with friends, family members, or coworkers to make it more enjoyable and motivating.
- Join a sports team, fitness class, or running group to meet new people and stay accountable to your fitness goals.

Incorporate movement into leisure activities:
- Choose leisure activities that involve physical movement, such as dancing, hiking, playing sports, or going for a bike ride.
- Instead of meeting friends for coffee or drinks, suggest going for a walk or participating in an active outing together.

Use technology to stay active:
- Use fitness apps, activity trackers, or wearable devices to monitor your physical activity and set goals for yourself.
- Follow online workout videos or streaming classes for guided exercise routines that you can do at home or while traveling.

Mix It Up:
- Keep your workouts varied and interesting by trying different types of exercises and activities.
- Incorporate a mix of cardiovascular exercise, strength training, flexibility exercises, and balance exercises to maintain overall fitness and prevent boredom.

Listen to Your Body:
- Pay attention to how your body feels during exercise and adjust your intensity or duration as needed.
- Rest and recover when necessary to prevent injury and allow your body to recover and rebuild.

Set realistic goals:
- Set achievable goals for yourself based on your current fitness level and lifestyle.
- Break larger goals into smaller, more manageable milestones to track your progress and stay motivated.

Stay Consistent:
- Consistency is key to seeing results and reaping the benefits of regular exercise.
- Make exercise a non-negotiable part of your daily routine, even on days when you don't feel like it.

Celebrate Your Successes:
- Acknowledge and celebrate your accomplishments, no matter how small.
- Reward yourself for reaching milestones and staying committed to your fitness journey.

Incorporating exercise and movement into your daily life is essential for maintaining physical health, improving mental well-being, and enhancing your overall quality of life. By scheduling regular workouts, staying active throughout the day, making exercise social, incorporating movement into leisure activities, using technology to stay active, mixing up your workouts, listening to your body, setting realistic goals, staying consistent, and celebrating your successes, you can create a sustainable and enjoyable exercise routine that supports your health and well-being in the long term.

Creating a Healthy Work-Life Balance

Creating a healthy work-life balance is essential for maintaining overall well-being and satisfaction in life. It involves finding the right equilibrium between your professional responsibilities and personal life, allowing you to fulfill your commitments at work while also making time for self-care, relaxation, and meaningful relationships.

To achieve a healthy work-life balance, it's important to set clear boundaries between work and personal time. This may involve establishing designated work hours and sticking to them, as well as resisting the temptation to bring work home or check emails outside of work hours. Creating a separate workspace at home, if possible, can also help reinforce these boundaries.

Prioritizing self-care is another key aspect of maintaining a healthy work-life balance. This includes getting enough sleep, eating nutritious meals, exercising regularly, and engaging in activities that bring you joy and relaxation. Making time for hobbies, interests, and social activities outside of work can help recharge your batteries and prevent burnout.

Communication is crucial to maintaining a healthy work-life balance, both with your employer and with your loved ones. Be transparent with your employer about your availability and boundaries, and don't hesitate to speak up if you're feeling overwhelmed or overworked. Similarly, communicate openly with your family and friends about your commitments and schedule, and make time for meaningful connections with loved ones.

Learning to manage your time effectively is also essential for achieving a healthy work-life balance. This may involve prioritizing tasks, setting realistic goals, and delegating responsibilities when necessary. It's important to be mindful of how you're spending your time and to make adjustments as needed to ensure that you're not neglecting important aspects of your life.

Finally, remember that achieving a healthy work-life balance is an ongoing process that requires regular reflection and adjustment. Be willing to reassess your priorities and make changes as needed to maintain balance and harmony in your life. By prioritizing self-care, setting boundaries, communicating effectively, managing your time wisely, and staying flexible, you can create a fulfilling and sustainable work-life balance that supports your overall well-being and happiness.

Setting Boundaries to Protect Your Energy

Setting boundaries to protect your energy is crucial for maintaining your emotional and mental well-being. Boundaries help define what is acceptable and unacceptable in your relationships, interactions, and daily life, allowing you to preserve your energy and prioritize your needs. Here's how you can set boundaries effectively:

Identify Your Limits:

- Take time to reflect on what drains your energy and causes stress or discomfort in your life.
- Identify situations, people, or behaviors that leave you feeling depleted, overwhelmed, or resentful.

Clarify Your Needs:

- Determine what you need to feel safe, respected, and supported in your relationships and interactions.
- Be clear about your personal boundaries and what is non-negotiable for you in terms of time, energy, and emotional resources.

Communicate assertively:

- Express your boundaries assertively and confidently, using clear and respectful language.
- Be direct and specific about what you will and will not tolerate, and communicate your needs and expectations openly.

Practice self-care:
- Prioritize self-care activities that nourish and replenish your energy, such as meditation, exercise, journaling, or spending time in nature.
- Make self-care a non-negotiable part of your routine, and don't feel guilty about taking time for yourself.

Learn to Say No:
- Practice saying no to requests, invitations, or obligations that don't align with your priorities or values.
- Remember that saying no is not selfish; it's an act of self-respect and self-preservation.

Set healthy boundaries:
- Establish clear boundaries around your time, space, and energy, and enforce them consistently.
- Be firm in your boundaries, even if others may push back or try to guilt-trip you into relenting.

Respect others' boundaries:
- Recognize and respect the boundaries of others, just as you expect them to respect yours.
- Avoid crossing boundaries or pressuring others to violate their own limits.

Be Prepared for Pushback:
- Understand that setting boundaries may be met with resistance or criticism from others, especially if they are used to disregarding your boundaries.

- Stay firm in your convictions, and don't let others manipulate or guilt-trip you into compromising your boundaries.

Seek support:
- Surround yourself with supportive individuals who respect and validate your boundaries.
- Seek guidance or support from a therapist, coach, or trusted friend or family member if you're struggling to set or enforce boundaries.

Practice self-compassion:
- Be kind and compassionate with yourself as you navigate setting and enforcing boundaries.
- Remember that setting boundaries is an act of self-love and self-care, and you deserve to protect your energy and well-being.

Setting boundaries to protect your energy is essential for maintaining your emotional and mental health. By identifying your limits, clarifying your needs, communicating assertively, practicing self-care, learning to say no, setting healthy boundaries, respecting others' boundaries, being prepared for pushback, seeking support, and practicing self-compassion, you can establish boundaries that honor your needs and priorities and create a healthier, more balanced life.

Developing a Nighttime Routine for Restful Sleep

Developing a nighttime routine for restful sleep is essential for promoting relaxation, unwinding from the day, and preparing your body and mind for a restorative night's rest. Here are some straight forward steps to help you establish a night time routine that supports healthy sleep:

Firstly, set a consistent bedtime and wake-up time, even on weekends, to regulate your body's internal clock and improve sleep quality. Aim to go to bed and wake up at the same time each day to establish a regular sleep-wake cycle.

Create a relaxing bedtime environment by dimming the lights, reducing noise, and minimizing distractions in your bedroom. Keep your bedroom cool, comfortable, and conducive to sleep by using blackout curtains, comfortable bedding, and a supportive mattress.

Avoid stimulating activities and electronic devices before bedtime, such as watching TV, using smartphones or tablets, or engaging in intense exercise. Instead, opt for calming activities that promote relaxation, such as reading a book, taking a warm bath, or practicing gentle yoga or meditation.

Limit caffeine and alcohol consumption in the evening, as these substances can interfere with your ability to fall asleep and stay asleep. Instead, opt for decaffeinated beverages or herbal teas that promote relaxation, such as chamomile or lavender tea.

Establish a soothing bedtime routine that signals to your body and mind that it's time to wind down and prepare for sleep. This may include activities such as listening to calming music, practicing deep breathing exercises, or writing in a gratitude journal.

Create a consistent pre-sleep ritual that helps you relax and transition from the busyness of the day to a state of restfulness. This could involve gentle stretching, progressive muscle relaxation, or visualizing peaceful and serene scenes.

Avoid heavy meals, spicy foods, and large amounts of liquids close to bedtime, as these can cause discomfort and disrupt sleep. Instead, opt for a light snack or herbal tea if you're hungry or thirsty before bed.

Limit exposure to bright lights, including screens from electronic devices, in the hour leading up to bedtime. Blue light emitted by screens can suppress the production of melatonin, a hormone that regulates sleep-wake cycles, making it harder to fall asleep.

Finally, practice patience and consistency as you establish your nighttime routine for restful sleep. It may take some time for your body and mind to adjust to the new habits and rhythms, so be gentle with yourself and give yourself grace as you prioritize your sleep health.

Developing a night time routine for restful sleep is essential for promoting relaxation, unwinding from the day, and preparing your body and mind for a restorative night's rest. By setting a consistent bedtime and wake-up time, creating a relaxing bedtime environment, avoiding stimulating activities and electronic devices before bedtime, limiting caffeine and alcohol consumption in the evening, establishing soothing bedtime rituals, creating a consistent pre-sleep routine, avoiding heavy meals and bright lights close to bedtime, and practicing patience and consistency, you can establish habits that support healthy sleep and overall well-being.

Chapter 6:
Triumph in Every Step

Celebrating Small Wins and Milestones

Celebrating small wins and milestones is a powerful way to acknowledge your progress, boost your confidence, and stay motivated on your journey toward achieving your goals. Here's how you can celebrate your accomplishments in a straight forward manner:

Firstly, recognize and appreciate the effort and dedication you put into reaching your goals, no matter how small or insignificant they may seem. Every step forward, no matter how small, is a step in the right direction toward success.

Acknowledge your achievements by taking a moment to reflect on the progress you've made and the obstacles you've overcome along the way. Celebrate the effort you've put in and the growth you've experienced, regardless of the outcome.

Share your successes with others, whether it's with friends, family, colleagues, or mentors. Allow yourself to bask in the praise and support of those who care about you and cheer you on in your endeavors.

Reward yourself for reaching milestones and achieving goals, whether it's with a small treat, a special outing, or a moment of relaxation and self-care. Acknowledge your hard work and dedication by indulging in something that brings you joy and satisfaction.

Keep track of your progress and accomplishments by maintaining a journal or log of your successes, no matter how big or small. Reflecting on your achievements can help you stay motivated and focused on your goals.

Celebrate the achievements of others as well, whether it's by congratulating a colleague on a job well done or supporting a friend in reaching their goals. By spreading positivity and encouragement, you contribute to a culture of success and mutual support.

Stay humble and gracious in your celebrations, recognizing that success is often the result of teamwork, support, and perseverance. Be grateful for the opportunities and resources that have helped you along the way, and pay it forward by supporting others in their journeys.

Celebrating small wins and milestones is an important part of achieving success and maintaining motivation. By recognizing your progress, acknowledging your achievements, sharing your successes with others, rewarding yourself, keeping track of your progress, celebrating the achievements of others, and staying humble and gracious in your celebrations, you can cultivate a mindset of positivity, resilience, and continuous growth on your journey toward success.

Acknowledging Your Progress and Growth

Acknowledging your progress and growth is a vital aspect of personal development and self-awareness. It involves recognizing the steps you've taken, the obstacles you've overcome, and the lessons you've learned along the way. Here's how you can acknowledge your progress and growth in a straightforward manner:

Firstly, take time to reflect on where you started and how far you've come. Consider the goals you set for yourself, the challenges you faced, and the progress you've made toward achieving them. Recognize the efforts you've put in and the improvements you've seen in yourself over time.

Celebrate the small victories and milestones you've reached along the way. Whether it's completing a task, reaching a goal, or overcoming a challenge, every achievement deserves recognition and praise. Acknowledge the hard work and dedication you've invested in yourself and your endeavors.

Be mindful of your strengths and accomplishments, no matter how insignificant they may seem. Recognize the skills you've developed, the knowledge you've gained, and the personal growth you've experienced through your efforts and experiences.

Acknowledge the setbacks and failures you've encountered as opportunities for growth and learning. Embrace the lessons they've taught you and the resilience they've helped you build. Understand that setbacks are a natural part of the journey toward success and that they can ultimately make you stronger and more resilient.

Seek feedback from others to gain perspective on your progress and growth. Listen to the observations and insights of friends, family members, mentors, and colleagues, and take their feedback into consideration as you assess your strengths and areas for improvement.

Keep track of your progress and achievements by maintaining a journal or log of your experiences. Document your successes, challenges, and lessons learned, and reflect on how they've shaped you as a person and contributed to your growth and development.

Stay committed to your personal growth journey by setting new goals and challenges for yourself. Continuously seek opportunities for learning, growth, and self-improvement, and embrace the challenges that come your way as opportunities to expand your horizons and reach your full potential.

Acknowledging your progress and growth is essential for fostering self-awareness, confidence, and personal development. By reflecting on your journey, celebrating your achievements, recognizing your strengths, learning from setbacks, seeking feedback, keeping track of your progress, and staying committed to your growth journey, you can cultivate a sense of fulfillment, resilience, and continuous improvement in your life.

Rewarding Yourself for Achievements

Rewarding yourself for achievements is a meaningful way to recognize your hard work, stay motivated, and celebrate your successes. It's important to acknowledge your efforts and accomplishments, no matter how big or small, and to take time to indulge in self-care and enjoyment. Here's how you can reward yourself for your achievements in a straightforward manner:

Firstly, identify your achievements, whether they're completing a project, reaching a milestone, or overcoming a challenge. Acknowledge the effort and dedication you put into achieving your goals and recognize the progress you've made.

Choose rewards that are meaningful and aligned with your interests, preferences, and values. Consider activities, experiences, or treats that bring you joy, relaxation, and fulfillment, such as treating yourself to a spa day, enjoying a favorite meal, or taking a day off to relax and recharge.

Set specific goals and milestones for yourself and establish rewards that correspond to each achievement. Having clear objectives and incentives can help keep you motivated and focused on your goals, and provide a sense of satisfaction and gratification when you reach them.

Practice self-compassion and avoid comparing yourself to others. Celebrate your achievements and successes, no matter how small, and recognize that progress is a journey, not a destination. Be kind to yourself and acknowledge the effort and dedication you put into reaching your goals.

Be consistent with rewarding yourself for your achievements, and make it a regular practice to celebrate your successes. Whether it's a weekly treat for meeting your goals or a special reward for reaching a major milestone, find ways to acknowledge and celebrate your progress along the way.

Incorporate rewards into your goal-setting process to provide additional motivation and incentive for achieving your objectives. By establishing rewards that are meaningful and aligned with your goals, you can stay motivated and focused on your objectives and enjoy the satisfaction of celebrating your successes along the way.

Rewarding yourself for achievements is a powerful way to recognize your hard work, stay motivated, and celebrate your successes. By acknowledging your efforts, choosing meaningful rewards, setting specific goals and milestones, practicing self-compassion, being consistent with rewarding yourself, and incorporating rewards into your goal-setting process, you can cultivate a sense of fulfillment, motivation, and satisfaction in your personal and professional endeavors.

Sharing Your Successes with Others

Sharing your successes with others is not only a way to celebrate your achievements but also an opportunity to inspire, motivate, and connect with those around you. Whether it's with friends, family, colleagues, or mentors, sharing your successes can foster a sense of camaraderie, support, and encouragement. Here's how you can share your successes with others in a straightforward manner:

Firstly, be proud of your accomplishments and don't hesitate to share them with those who care about you. Whether it's a personal achievement, a professional milestone, or something in between, don't downplay your successes or feel the need to minimize them. Embrace your achievements and celebrate them openly.

Choose the right moment and setting to share your successes with others. Whether it's over a cup of coffee, during a casual conversation, or in a formal setting, consider the context and dynamics of the situation, and choose a time and place where you feel comfortable and confident sharing your achievements.

Be genuine and authentic when sharing your successes with others. Share your experiences, challenges, and lessons learned along the way, and be open about the hard work, dedication, and sacrifices that went into achieving your goals. Avoid bragging or exaggerating your accomplishments, and instead, focus on sharing your journey in a humble and relatable manner.

Express gratitude and appreciation for the support and encouragement you've received from others along the way. Acknowledge the role that friends, family, colleagues, mentors, and others have played in your success, and express your gratitude for their contributions to your journey.

Be mindful of how you share your successes, especially in professional or competitive settings. While it's important to celebrate your achievements, be sensitive to the feelings and experiences of others and avoid coming across as boastful or insensitive. Focus on inspiring and uplifting others rather than seeking validation or recognition.

Celebrate the successes of others as well, and be generous with your praise and support. By celebrating the achievements of those around you, you contribute to a culture of positivity, encouragement, and mutual support and strengthen your relationships with others.

Sharing your successes with others is a powerful way to celebrate your achievements, inspire those around you, and strengthen your connections with others. By being proud of your accomplishments, choosing the right moment and setting to share your successes, being genuine and authentic, expressing gratitude and appreciation, being mindful of how you share your successes, celebrating the successes of others, and fostering a culture of positivity and support, you can share your successes in a way that inspires, motivates, and uplifts those around you.

Learning from Setbacks and Challenges

Learning from setbacks and challenges is an essential part of personal and professional growth. While setbacks can be frustrating and disheartening, they also present valuable opportunities for learning, resilience, and self-improvement. Here's how you can learn from setbacks and challenges in a straightforward manner:

Firstly, acknowledge and accept the setback or challenge you've encountered. Avoid denying or minimizing the situation, and instead, face it head-on with a sense of acceptance and willingness to learn from the experience.

Reflect on the factors that contributed to the setback or challenge. Consider what went wrong, what could have been done differently, and what lessons can be gleaned from the experience. Be honest with yourself and take responsibility for your role in the situation.

Identify the lessons learned from the setback or challenge. Consider how the experience has helped you grow, develop new skills, or gain valuable insights. Look for silver linings and positive takeaways that can be applied to future situations.

Use setbacks and challenges as opportunities for self-reflection and introspection. Take time to evaluate your strengths, weaknesses, and areas for improvement, and consider how you can build on your strengths and address your weaknesses moving forward.

Seek feedback from others to gain different perspectives on the situation. Consult friends, family members, colleagues, mentors, or other trusted individuals for their insights and advice on how to learn from the setback or challenge and grow from the experience.

Develop a plan of action for moving forward. Based on the lessons learned and insights gained from the setback or challenge, create actionable steps for overcoming obstacles, achieving goals, and improving outcomes in the future. Set realistic and achievable goals, and stay committed to continuous improvement and growth.

Stay resilient in the face of setbacks and challenges. Embrace failure as a natural part of the learning process and use setbacks as opportunities to bounce back stronger and more determined than before. Cultivate a mindset of perseverance, resilience, and optimism, and keep pushing forward despite obstacles and setbacks.

Learning from setbacks and challenges is a valuable opportunity for personal and professional growth. By acknowledging setbacks, reflecting on lessons learned, seeking feedback, developing a plan of action, staying resilient, and embracing failure as a learning opportunity, you can turn setbacks into stepping stones toward success and become a stronger, wiser, and more resilient individual in the process.

Cultivating Resilience and Perseverance in the Face of Adversity

Cultivating resilience and perseverance in the face of adversity is essential for overcoming challenges, bouncing back from setbacks, and achieving success.

<u>Here are some straightforward strategies to help you develop resilience and perseverance:</u>

Maintain a Positive Outlook:

- Focus on the aspects of the situation that you can control rather than dwelling on what you can't.
- Look for silver linings and opportunities for growth and learning in every challenge you face.
- Practice gratitude and mindfulness to cultivate a positive mindset and reduce stress.

Build a Support System:

- Surround yourself with friends, family members, colleagues, mentors, and other supportive individuals who can provide encouragement, guidance, and emotional support.
- Don't hesitate to reach out for help when you need it, and be willing to offer support to others in return.

Develop Coping Strategies:

- Identify healthy coping mechanisms that help you manage stress, anxiety, and other negative emotions.

This could include activities such as exercise, meditation, journaling, or spending time in nature.
- Practice self-care regularly to recharge your batteries and maintain your physical, mental, and emotional well-being.

Set Realistic Goals:
- Break larger goals down into smaller, more manageable tasks that you can tackle one step at a time.
- Celebrate small victories along the way to stay motivated and reinforce your sense of progress and achievement.

Learn from Failure:
- Embrace failure as a natural part of the learning process and an opportunity for growth and improvement.
- Analyze what went wrong and what you can do differently next time to increase your chances of success.
- Use setbacks as valuable learning experiences that help you become stronger, more resilient, and more resourceful in the long run.

Adapt to Change:
- Be flexible and open-minded in your approach to challenges, and be willing to adapt your strategies and plans as needed.
- Recognize that change is inevitable and that your ability to adapt to new circumstances is key to overcoming adversity.

Stay Persistent:

- Don't give up in the face of obstacles or setbacks. Instead, stay committed to your goals and keep pushing forward, even when the going gets tough.
- Remember that perseverance is often the key to success, and that setbacks are temporary roadblocks on the path to achievement.

By cultivating resilience and perseverance in the face of adversity, you can develop the strength, determination, and resilience needed to overcome challenges and achieve your goals. Remember to maintain a positive outlook, build a strong support system, develop healthy coping strategies, set realistic goals, learn from failure, adapt to change, and stay persistent in pursuing your dreams.

Chapter 7:
Faith in Action

Exploring Different Forms of Faith and Spirituality

Exploring different forms of faith and spirituality can be a deeply enriching and fulfilling journey that allows individuals to connect with something greater than themselves and find meaning and purpose in life. Here's how you can approach exploring different forms of faith and spirituality in a straightforward manner:

Open-Mindedness and Curiosity:

- Approach the exploration of faith and spirituality with an open mind and a willingness to learn about different beliefs, practices, and traditions.
- Be curious and inquisitive, seeking out opportunities to explore various religious and spiritual paths without judgment or preconceived notions.

Research and study:

- Take the time to research and study different religions, spiritual practices, and philosophical traditions to gain a better understanding of their beliefs, teachings, and rituals.

- Utilize resources such as books, articles, documentaries, and online resources to delve into the rich tapestry of faith and spirituality.

Attend religious services and gatherings:

- Attend religious services, ceremonies, and gatherings of different faith traditions to experience firsthand the rituals, prayers, and community aspects of various religions.
- Participate in spiritual retreats, workshops, and events that offer opportunities for personal growth, reflection, and connection with others on a spiritual journey.

Engage in dialogue and discussion.

- Engage in open and respectful dialogue with individuals from diverse religious and spiritual backgrounds to gain insights into their beliefs, experiences, and perspectives.
- Seek out opportunities for interfaith dialogue and collaboration to foster understanding, respect, and cooperation among people of different faiths and traditions.

Reflect and internalize:

- Take time for introspection and reflection to discern what resonates with you personally and spiritually.
- Reflect on your own beliefs, values, and experiences, and consider how they align with different religious and spiritual teachings and practices.

Seek guidance and mentorship.

- Seek guidance and mentorship from spiritual leaders, teachers, or mentors who can offer support, guidance, and wisdom on your spiritual journey.
- Be open to receiving guidance and insights from trusted spiritual advisors who can help you navigate the complexities of faith and spirituality.

By approaching the exploration of different forms of faith and spirituality with an open mind, a spirit of curiosity, and a commitment to personal growth, you can embark on a transformative journey of self-discovery, connection, and spiritual fulfillment. Remember to engage in research and study, attend religious services and gatherings, engage in dialogue and discussion, reflect and internalize, practice mindfulness and meditation, and seek guidance and mentorship as you explore the rich diversity of faith and spirituality.

Finding Strength and Comfort in Prayer and Meditation

Finding strength and comfort in prayer and meditation is a deeply personal and meaningful practice for many individuals. It provides a way to connect with a higher power, whether that be through religious beliefs or spiritual connection, and offers solace, guidance, and inner peace in times of difficulty or uncertainty.

Prayer, often associated with religious traditions, involves communicating with a divine entity or higher power. It can take many forms, including reciting scripted prayers, expressing gratitude, making requests for guidance or assistance, or simply engaging in heartfelt conversation with a deity or spiritual force.

For those who practice prayer, it serves as a source of strength, hope, and comfort, providing reassurance in times of adversity and a sense of connection to something greater than oneself. Many people find solace in the belief that their prayers are heard and that they are not alone in facing life's challenges.

Meditation, on the other hand, is a secular practice that focuses on mindfulness, self-awareness, and inner peace. It involves quieting the mind, focusing on the present moment, and observing thoughts and emotions without judgment. Meditation techniques can vary widely, ranging from focused breathing exercises to guided imagery or body scan practices.

Through meditation, individuals can cultivate a sense of calm, clarity, and resilience, enabling them to navigate life's ups and downs with greater ease and equanimity. By quieting the chatter of the mind and turning inward, meditation offers a refuge from the stresses and distractions of daily life, allowing individuals to tap into their inner wisdom and intuition.

Whether through prayer, meditation, or a combination of both, finding strength and comfort in spiritual practices can be a powerful tool for coping with life's challenges. It provides a sense of purpose, meaning, and connection to something larger than oneself, fostering resilience, hope, and inner peace in the face of adversity.

Ultimately, the practice of prayer and meditation is deeply personal and individualized, with each person finding their own unique path to spiritual connection and inner peace. By exploring different forms of faith and spirituality, individuals can discover what resonates most deeply with them and cultivate a practice that brings them strength, comfort, and solace in times of need.

Trusting in Divine Timing and Universal Guidance

Trusting in divine timing and universal guidance is a belief that everything happens for a reason and that there is a greater plan unfolding beyond our control. It involves surrendering to the notion that there is a higher power at work in the universe, orchestrating events, and guiding us along our path in life.

For many individuals, trusting in divine timing means having faith that things will unfold as they are meant to, even if they don't happen according to our own timeline or desires. It requires letting go of the need to control every aspect of our lives and instead surrendering to the flow of life, trusting that the universe has our best interests at heart.

This belief can provide comfort and reassurance in times of uncertainty or difficulty, knowing that we are not alone and that there is greater wisdom guiding us through life's twists and turns. It allows us to release the burden of worry and anxiety, trusting that everything will work out in the end.

Trusting in divine timing also means being open to receiving guidance from the universe, whether through signs, intuition, or synchronicities. It involves paying attention to the subtle cues and messages that the universe sends our way and following our inner guidance, even if it goes against conventional logic or societal expectations.

By trusting in divine timing and universal guidance, we can find peace, purpose, and meaning in the midst of life's challenges and uncertainties. It allows us to surrender to the flow of life, trusting that everything is unfolding exactly as it should and that we are being guided toward our highest good.

Ultimately, trusting in divine timing is a deeply personal and individual belief, shaped by our own experiences, beliefs, and values. It is a practice that requires faith, patience, and surrender, but it can bring profound peace, clarity, and alignment with the greater purpose of our lives.

Letting Go of Control and Surrendering to the Flow of Life

Letting go of control and surrendering to the flow of life is a transformative practice that involves releasing the need to micromanage every aspect of our lives and instead trusting in the natural unfolding of events. It requires relinquishing the illusion of control and embracing a mindset of acceptance, flexibility, and openness to whatever life brings our way.

For many people, letting go of control can be challenging, as it often goes against our natural inclination to plan, organize, and strive for certainty and predictability. However, the reality is that life is inherently unpredictable and constantly changing, and trying to control every outcome only leads to frustration, stress, and resistance.

Surrendering to the flow of life means acknowledging that there are forces at work beyond our understanding and that there is wisdom in accepting things as they are, rather than constantly trying to force them to conform to our expectations. It involves trusting in the universe, or a higher power, to guide us and knowing that we are supported and protected, even in the face of uncertainty.

Letting go of control doesn't mean giving up or being passive. Instead, it means surrendering the need to control every outcome and instead focusing on what we can control—our thoughts, attitudes, and actions. It means being proactive rather than reactive and responding to life's challenges with resilience, adaptability, and grace.

By letting go of control and surrendering to the flow of life, we open ourselves up to new possibilities, opportunities, and experiences that we may have never imagined. We learn to trust in our own intuition and inner wisdom and to follow the path that feels right for us, even if it doesn't always make sense to others.

Ultimately, letting go of control and surrendering to the flow of life is a deeply transformative practice that can lead to greater peace, fulfillment, and joy. It allows us to release the burden of trying to control every outcome and instead embrace the beauty and mystery of life's journey, trusting that everything is unfolding exactly as it should.

Finding Meaning and Purpose in Life's Challenges

Finding meaning and purpose in life's challenges is a profound journey of self-discovery and growth. While facing difficulties and setbacks may seem daunting, they also offer valuable opportunities for personal development, resilience, and finding deeper fulfillment in life. Here are some straightforward strategies to help you find meaning and purpose in life's challenges:

Reflect on your values and beliefs:

- Take time to reflect on what truly matters to you and what you believe in.
- Consider how your values and beliefs can guide you through difficult times and help you find meaning in adversity.

Search for lessons and growth opportunities.

- View challenges as opportunities for learning, growth, and self-improvement.
- Look for the lessons that can be gleaned from difficult experiences and use them as stepping stones toward personal development.

Connect with others:

- Seek support from friends, family members, or support groups that can offer empathy, encouragement, and perspective.
- Share your experiences with others and learn from their insights and experiences.

Find purpose in helping others:
- Look for ways to contribute to the well-being of others, whether through acts of kindness, volunteering, or supporting a cause you believe in.
- Finding purpose in helping others can provide a sense of fulfillment and meaning, even in the midst of personal challenges.

Embrace resilience and adaptability.
- Cultivate resilience by facing challenges with courage, determination, and optimism.
- Embrace adaptability by being flexible and open-minded in your approach to adversity and by finding creative solutions to overcome obstacles.

Focus on What You Can Control:
- Focus on the aspects of the situation that you can control, such as your attitude, actions, and responses.
- Let go of the need to control external circumstances and instead focus on how you can navigate challenges with grace and resilience.

Seek Meaning in Small Moments of Joy and Gratitude:
- Find meaning in everyday moments of joy, beauty, and gratitude.
- Cultivate a practice of mindfulness and appreciation for the simple pleasures in life, even in the midst of difficult times.

By following these strategies, you can navigate life's challenges with resilience, optimism, and a sense of purpose.

Remember that challenges are a natural part of the human experience and that finding meaning and purpose in adversity is a powerful way to transform difficult experiences into opportunities for growth and fulfillment.

Connecting with a Community of Like-Minded Individuals for Support and Encouragement

Connecting with a community of like-minded individuals can provide invaluable support, encouragement, and camaraderie during challenging times. Whether you're facing personal struggles, pursuing ambitious goals, or simply seeking companionship, being part of a supportive community can make a significant difference in your well-being and overall outlook on life.

When you connect with a community of like-minded individuals, you're joining a network of people who share similar interests, values, and aspirations. This sense of belonging can foster a deep sense of connection and understanding, as well as a shared sense of purpose and mutual support.

One of the key benefits of being part of a like-minded community is the opportunity to receive support and encouragement from others who understand what you're going through. Whether you're dealing with a specific challenge or simply need a listening ear, knowing that you're not alone can provide comfort and reassurance during difficult times.

In addition to receiving support, being part of a community allows you to offer support to others who may be facing similar struggles. By sharing your own experiences, insights, and words of encouragement, you can make a positive impact on the lives of others and contribute to the overall well-being of the community.

Being part of a like-minded community also provides opportunities for collaboration, learning, and personal growth. Whether through participating in group discussions, attending workshops and events, or collaborating on projects, you can expand your knowledge, skills, and perspective in a supportive and nurturing environment.

Finally, being part of a community of like-minded individuals can provide a sense of accountability and motivation to stay focused on your goals and aspirations. Knowing that others are cheering you on and rooting for your success can inspire you to persevere in the face of obstacles and strive for excellence in all areas of your life.

In conclusion, connecting with a community of like-minded individuals can be a powerful source of support, encouragement, and inspiration during challenging times. Whether you're seeking emotional support, personal growth, or simply companionship, being part of a supportive community can make a positive difference in your life and help you navigate life's ups and downs with greater resilience and optimism.

CONCLUSION

In conclusion, "Resilience Beyond Adversity - Harnessing Motivation For Personal Growth" is more than just a book; it's a roadmap to living a more fulfilling and resilient life. Throughout these pages, you've explored the power of mindset, the importance of resilience, and the value of embracing challenges as opportunities for growth.

As you close this book, remember that personal growth is a journey, not a destination. It requires dedication, patience, and a willingness to step outside of your comfort zone. But with the strategies and insights you've gained from "Resilience Beyond Adversity," you're equipped to face whatever challenges come your way with courage and determination.

Continue to cultivate a positive mindset, lean on your support system, and stay committed to your goals. Remember that setbacks are a natural part of the process, and each one presents an opportunity for learning and growth. Trust in yourself and the journey you're on, and never forget the incredible potential that lies within you.

Thank you for joining me on this journey of discovery and empowerment. May you continue to unlock your potential and live a life filled with purpose, resilience, and joy.

Author Biography

Enzo Leonardo, a charismatic and devoted family man deeply rooted in his faith, exudes a fervent dedication to empowering others to triumph over adversity. His own life journey compelled him to confront daunting challenges, pushing him to explore the depths of his

resilience. Through these trials, Enzo unearthed the transformative power of motivation and personal growth. Inspired by his experiences, he authored "Resilience Beyond Adversity -

Harnessing Motivation for Personal Growth," a testament to his unyielding determination to support others on their path to success. With seven chapters brimming with insights, Enzo's book serves as a beacon of guidance, inviting readers to cultivate their inner strength, surmount obstacles, and flourish amidst life's challenges. Enzo's sincere desire to uplift others resonates throughout his work, offering a valuable companion for those embarking on their journey toward resilience and personal growth.

www.ingramcontent.com/pod-product-compliance
Lightning Source LLC
Chambersburg PA
CBHW050323230526
45471CB00005B/2331